Contents

The POWER of PRAISE

by
Kenneth
Erickson

Publishing House
St. Louis

Copyright © 1984 Concordia Publishing House
3558 South Jefferson Avenue
St. Louis, Missouri 63118

Printed in the United States of America

Library of Congress Cataloging in Publication Data

Erickson, Kenneth A.
    The power of praise.

    1. Self-respect. 2. Christian life—1960— 3. Praise. I. Title.

BJ1533.S3E75   1984   248.4   83-23968
ISBN 0-570-03925-8

---

1 2 3 4 5 6 7 8 9 10   DB   93 92 91 90 89 88 87 86 85 84

Acknowledgments

This book is dedicated to all my former students and co-workers who taught me the importance of praise in interpersonal relationships. Particular acknowledgment is offered to John Casteel, teacher, friend, and mentor who in his quiet way effectively embodies the best examples in this book.

Special appreciation is expressed to my parents for their close walk with God, a primary influence in the direction of my life.

Extraordinary friends who have shared some of their experiences effectively illustrating important concepts in the book include Don Bartlette, Agnes Best, Ron Burge, Leo and Signe Bustad, Dick Carignan, Donald Clifton, John Craig, Rolf Erickson, Betty and Larry Fish, Vince Gallo, Bob Grover, Mike Johnson, Steve Lauch, Karen McIntyre, Merle Ohlsen, Roger Rada, Mel Roberts, Emily Samuels, Fenton Sharpe, Bernice Skinner, Bob Stalick, Annette Stixrud, Wes Sullivan, Bob and Carol Taylor, Jim Thiessen, and Roy Vernstrom.

In addition, I thank Doc Streator for his valuable research and suggestions for portions of the book, as well as Linda Gill for her cheerful and careful manuscript typing.

Finally, I thank my wife, Lois, without whose loving counsel, patience, and understanding such projects would never be completed.

Introduction

*. . . if there be any excellence,
if there is anything worthy of praise,
think about these things.*
Philippians 4:8

In a country church in a small European village an altar boy serving the priest at a Sunday mass accidentally dropped the cruet of wine. The village priest struck the boy sharply on the head and in an angry voice commanded, "Leave this altar and don't ever come back!" Later the boy became Marshall Tito of Yugoslavia.

In a cathedral of a large city another altar boy serving the bishop at a Sunday mass dropped the cruet of wine. With a warm twinkle in his eye the bishop gently whispered, "Someday you will be a priest." Later the boy became Archbishop Fulton Sheen.

The results of affirming (encouraging, appreciating, praising) or of infirming (reproaching, belittling, criticizing) seldom are as clearcut as in the story of the two altar boys. Yet every interpersonal relationship in which we engage is one unit of our cumulative effect on other individuals and on the world—for better or for worse.

Figure 1 simplifies this thought and illustrates three elements basic to the book's central theme. (1) A review of common terms descriptive of human interactions reveals more than twice as many negative or infirming terms as positive or affirming terms. (2) Studies of the number of infirming statements in contrast to affirming statements made suggest that we use terms from the negative list far more frequently than from the positive list. One study (see page 99) reveals a ratio of nine infirming comments to one affirming comment. (3) The balance arm in Figure 1 appears to be tilted in the wrong direction, since one negative unit is

9

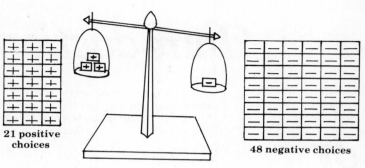

Figure 1

21 positive choices

48 negative choices

Possibilities for Affirming Others	Possibilities for Infirming Others		
Accepting	Admonishing	Dressing Down	Reproaching
Acclaiming	Assailing	Finding Fault	Ripping Into
Admiring	Avoiding	Harassing	Scolding
Approving	Bawling Out	Jumping Down One's Throat	Slapping One's Wrists
Appreciating	Belittling		
Cherishing	Berating	Knocking	Slighting
Commending	Blaming	Laughing At	Taking to Task
Congratulating	Blistering	Laying the Blame On	Telling Off
Encouraging	Calling Down		Tongue Lashing
Exalting	Calling on Carpet	Mistreating	Upbraiding
Holding dear	Castigating	Negating	Writing Off
Honoring	Censuring	Neglecting	
Loving	Chastening	Panning	
Patting on back	Chewing Out	Picking to Pieces	
Praising	Condemning	Raking over the Coals	
Recommending	Criticizing		
Regarding well	Denouncing	Reading the Riot Act to	
Recognizing	Depreciating	Reaming Out	
Respecting	Disapproving	Rejecting	
Supporting	Discouraging	Reprimanding	
Wishing well	Disparaging		

10

shown as outweighing three positive units. Yet most of us assign significantly more weight to one negative comment we hear than to several positive comments. For example, I once accepted a certificate awarding me "ONE ATTABOY FOR OUTSTANDING PERFORMANCE." The inscription continued, "One thousand Attaboys qualify you to be a recognized leader, work overtime with a smile, and explain assorted problems to your boss. Note: One "AWSHUX" wipes the board clean and you start all over again!" Leo Buscaglia supports this thinking in his book *Living, Loving, and Learning,* where he writes,

People can tell us all day long that we are wondrous and marvelous, and we are worthy of all kinds of things. Then one person will tell us that he doesn't like us, and we are destroyed.[1]

Most of us remain unmindful of the tremendous power we have when affirming or infirming individuals. Our positive example, however, can influence others to increase affirmations of those they meet. Suppose, for example, that I affirmed two individuals one day and that each one was motivated to affirm two others the next day. *If* this process continued, more than 120 persons would be affirmed on day seven, 16,000 on day 14, and 2,000,000 on day 21. Of course, the same progression applies to the act of infirming. Regardless of whether we praise or belittle, we can't envision where our impact on the lives of others may end.

Self-esteem depends heavily on whether we are recognized or ignored, respected or ridiculed, praised or belittled. Too often we are dehumanized by blaming and shaming, by ridiculing and admonishing. What we need is a person who will come up to us, put an arm on our shoulder, and in all sincerity say "I appreciate you and the effective way you are handling your responsibility." Lacking that, however, we should never overlook the explicit promises of God's love for us. Peter is helpful as he assures us

Once you were less than nothing; now you are God's own. Once you knew little of God's kindness; now your very lives have been changed by it. (1 Peter 2:10, TLB)

The Power of Praise deals with the amazing potential for good each of us has in the lives of others. It also examines the destructive consequences of infirming words and actions which counteract our most positive intentions. In analyzing the contrasting results of affirming and infirming forces, we will gain a clearer understanding of the normally negelected potential of praise.

In this book you will meet leaders, workers, supervisors, parents, youth, the elderly, and the imprisoned. Their experiences will demonstrate that one to the deepest principles of our nature is the desire for appreciation, the need to receive genuine praise.

How many persons do we ignore at home, at work, at worship who deserve and yearn for loving recognition? We have ignored our potential as positive influences in the lives of others too long. I pray that this book will kindle your desire to utilize the potential of affirming praise in the lives of your family, friends, and co-workers.

Arthur Gordon's prayer describes my perspective as I worked on this book.

Lord of all things, whose wondrous gifts to man
Include the shining symbols known as words,
Grant that I may use their mighty power
Only for good. Help me to pass on
Small fragments of Your wisdom, truth, and love.
Open my ears, my eyes, unlock my heart,
Speak through me, Lord, if it be Your will.

1
Praise, Indifference, and Criticism

The deepest principle of human nature
is the craving to be appreciated.
William James

*B*ess Curry was my high school physics teacher. She was single, close to 50 years old, bantam in size, but sturdy in spirit. Her rectangular glasses slid down a little on her nose. They matched her square jaw and ever present wide smile. She was devoted to teaching and committed to helping students.

I was a shy senior. Miss Curry must have seen me as a special challenge. She bolstered my self-confidence with, "Kenneth, I'd like you to do these advanced assignments." Before school, during class, or after school her unconditional acceptance melted away my feelings of worthlessness. Gradually her praise and her trust overruled my self-doubting. I learned firsthand of Solomon's wisdom in Proverbs 16:24: "Pleasant words are like a honeycomb, sweetness to the soul and health to the body."

Bess Curry had high expectations for her students. She attempted to challenge every student's maximum potential. Though no one in my family ever had enrolled in college, she decreed, "Kenneth, you have the ability to succeed in college." Miss Curry's assured attitude strengthened my self-confidence. How could I doubt the advice of an adult who really cared about me, expressed confidence in my ability, praised my work, and challenged my potential? Her positive words and support changed my whole life. Bless the memory of the Bess Currys in our lives!

INDIFFERENCE INJURES

The worst sin toward our fellow creatures is not to hate them, but to be indifferent to them.
George Bernard Shaw

*T*he enhancing power of praise is the central theme of this book. To understand the importance of positive affirmations, however, the theme will be highlighted by contrasts against a backdrop of indifference and criticism.

Joyce Landorf gives an example of how adults can be indifferent to their children who yearn for parental recognition and praise. In her book, *Irregular Persons*, she writes of a father who was told by many people that his daughter was especially talented in piano and voice, but whenever she performed in musicals or gave recitals, he never attended. Even after she had excelled in music and had several solo albums to her credit, his only observation to her was, "You should hear Mrs. Brown play the piano . . . because she can *really* play!" How painful for his own daughter who yearned for her father's recognition and praise.[1]

A graduate student related the following about his dad. "My father probably was the most profound influence on my early life. He *never* affirmed me openly . . . . Praise to my face would have stuck in his throat."

During my childhood I too felt that my dad was indifferent to me. I concluded, "right or wrong," that he did not love me. Yet I yearned for Dad's hugs; I wanted to sit on his lap and have him hold me just like he would hold my sister.

He died when I was 17, before we had a chance to develop a more mature understanding. Today I believe that he wanted to love me and did the best he knew how. Now I can see Dad as a fellow human being, struggling but falling short of his goals even as I do. Paul understood us both when he wrote, "My own behavior baffles me. For I find myself doing what I really loathe and not doing what I really want to do" (Romans 7:15, Phillips). As my fellow struggler, Dad has become understandable to me. He struggled with the challenge of living in a Swedish culture his first 17 years, where obedience to adult discipline took priority over family warmth. His ability to express love to me was consistent

14

with the love or lack thereof he experienced in his childhood home.

CRITICISM DISABLES

Our worst fault is our preoccupation
with the faults of others.
Kahlil Gibran

*H*ow prevalent is the attempt to raise my own self-concept by comparing my faults to the failings of others. The greater my faults, the more I seem concerned with the imperfections of others. A Malaysian proverb asserts that we can see a louse in China but we are unconscious of an elephant on our own nose.

In *The Meaning of Persons*, Paul Tournier says that people are quick to pass judgment; they break the beginner's spirit by pointing out his smallest blunders; they maintain their self-confidence by decrying those who have real talent.[2] It is difficult for us to escape from jealousies that so quickly prompt us to criticize.

Many of us betray ourselves by the criticisms we make of others. If I am critical of a fellow church member who always is at the front of the line at potluck dinners, that may reveal my own "me-first" attitude. It has been said that none of us can stand other people having the same faults as ourselves. Our tolerance is especially challenged when our own children display the same qualities to which we object in ourselves. At times I've felt one of our children must have been intentionally taunting me with traits I most disliked in myself. These were negative qualities that I had been unable to overcome. Our child's actions needled me where I was most vulnerable. I found it difficult to be positive and understanding under such pressure. According to Jules Renhard, "When the defects of others are perceived with so much clarity, it is because one possesses them oneself."

I believe the child most like one parent has the most difficulty being accepted, loved, and praised by that parent. Though my father died when I was 17 years old, I concluded years ago that I must have inherited several traits from him that he disliked in himself.

When I was a boy our family attended Sunday evening services each week in the basement fellowship hall of our

15

church. Squirming through an hour of song and message on a hard bench was not easy. Some of my best buddies were there also, storing up restless energy while waiting to be released by the final "Amen."

Our sprint by the refreshment table barely gave us time to grab a few cookies. Then we charged out to vent our energies in running, whooping, and playing hide-and-seek. Occasionally we would make a daring dash down the long aisle of the unlit sanctuary upstairs. The dim EXIT light in the back was more eerie than illuminating on our exciting run through church. Our fun reached its peak when some of us ventured to hide between the pews. Jumping out to scare a friend racing through the dark would bring howls of surprise.

What was holy hilarity for youth, however, could border on desecration for parents who wished to pride themselves in their child's public behavior. In any event, Dad's verdict as we left church was final. "You're due for a hard spanking when you get home!" At those times I wondered how anything so joyous as playing at church could be so wrong.

One by-product of being regularly infirmed is that individuals lose confidence in themselves. Eventually we can reject ourselves as Moses devalued himself when God called him for a special assignment. Several times Moses replied, "I am nobody. How can I go to the king and bring the Israelites out of Egypt?" Another time he depreciated himself with, "No, Lord, don't send me. I am a poor speaker, slow and hesitant." Feelings of inferiority and low self-esteem sabotage our self-confidence and impair healthy relationships with employers, family, and friends.

An analysis of my childhood and youth made me realize the superabundance of infirming techniques available to humankind. We can criticize, punish, belittle, find fault, laugh at, discourage, neglect, discredit, or reject other persons. With a few words we can either build up or beat down another's self-esteem. While careless words or acts cause them to feel rejected, deserved praise and loving actions help others to gain self-respect and dignity.

My Aunt Edith and Uncle Gus were two of the most affirming and positive persons I have known. As a youth I mowed and trimmed their lawn for them during summer. Just as if it were yesterday, I still can hear my aunt calling to her husband, "Gus, come out in front and see what Kenny

16

has done. He found and uncovered all our stepping stones between the street and the sidewalk!" I lapped up every word. How I relished her praise. I worked harder than ever to please such appreciative employers.

How can we learn to observe good traits in others? In *The Friendship Factor* Alan McGinnis advises

If you train your mind to search for positive things about other people, you will be surprised at how many good things you can observe in them and comment upon.[3]

Unfortunately, we are prone to postpone affirming others. Understanding this, Paul advised us to fill our minds "with those things that are good and that deserve praise...." (Phil. 4:8, TEV). He knew that sporadic efforts sabotage good intentions.

While we struggle with imagined or real hurts from someone who has treated us with indifference or criticism, we are often blind to the affirmations available in God's plan of salvation, which are valid affirmations of substance. Peter tells us, ". . . you are a chosen people, a royal priesthood, a holy nation, a people belonging to God, that you may declare the praises of Him who called you out of darkness into His wonderful light" (1 Peter 2:9, NIV). Jesus tells us "I am the good shepherd.... I know my sheep.... And I am willing to die for them" (John 14:14-15, TEV). Again He says, "You didn't choose me; I chose you, and appointed you to go and bear much fruit, the kind of fruit that endures" (John 15: 16, TEV). Such affirmations to those who accept God's love will undergird them in every facet of their lives.

A LOOK AHEAD

We might not take so much comfort in another person's imperfections if we didn't have so many faults ourselves.

*A*ccording to Bruce Larson (*Living on the Growing Edge*), there are four basic attitudes that persons have toward others.
1. We can be indifferent.
2. We can flatter.
3. We can criticize.
4. We can be affirming.[4]

When we are indifferent to others they feel of little worth. Indifference is the opposite of love and often destructive. If we attempt to flatter we are exploitive, manipulative, and actually self-serving rather than other-serving. The third possible attitude is criticism. Criticism from friends can be helpful if we request their assistance. Unrequested criticisms, however, vary from discouraging to devastating. The fourth possible attitude is affirmation. When our affirmation or praise is sincere, it builds another person's self-esteem. It often brings to light positive qualities of which the affirmed person is unaware.

My interest in the power of praise and the negative power of reproach grew more from my struggles than from successes. The thoughts in this book germinated slowly during years of personal interactions while working as employment manager in industry, principal in a city high school, superintendent of schools, and college professor. More recently I have tested and refined my thinking on interpersonal relationships during interactions with participants in several hundred management seminars.

This book suggests how we can be a positive force in evoking a positive transforming spirit in other persons. First, we will deal with overcoming inclinations to *infirm* others by reproaching and belittling them. Second, we will work on overcoming our reluctance to *affirm* others—to communicate our trust, appreciation, and praise. A primary purpose is to transform our day-to-day relationships with others so that our lives will be more consistent with Proverbs 3:27, "Do not withhold good from those to whom it is due."

2
Self-Confidence: How do You Rate?

As is our confidence, so is our capacity.
William Hazlitt

I asked participants at an adult discussion session how many of them felt adequate and self-confident. No one raised a hand. Even if a few of them felt reasonably capable, not one felt assured enough to admit it publicly. Most adults are handicapped by a small self-concept. The participants felt inadequate; they probably underestimated their God-given potential.

Low self-esteem as reported by the discussion participants restricts their accomplishments. Even though completely adequate for a given task, their reduced self-confidence convinces them they are inadequate.

The discussion participants were comparing themselves unfavorably to an inflated estimate of the self-confidence level of others. They prejudged themselves inferior by comparison. When low self-confidence controls our lives, we limit the extent to which our God-given abilities can be used in His service. A card on my desk addresses this situation. It says, "Use whatever talent you have. How silent the woods would be if only the best birds sang."

God has given each of us some special abilities. Low self-confidence downgrades these gifts. Fearful of failure or of looking foolish, we bury our talents. We often are unaware of some abilities that God expects us to use. Nathaniel Branden wrote in his book *The Disowned Self:* "Nothing is easier than for men to practice self-renunciation;

19

they do so every day; it is not a difficult feat or a moral achievement; it is a disease."[1]

While we all have a need to be needed, women suffer from lack of self-esteem more than men. In one study 50 percent of the women selected low self-esteem as their number one problem. Eighty percent of them ranked it in the top five of all their problems.

CONFIDENCE-METER DISCREPANCIES

Some of us have an "indoor-outdoor" thermometer at home. We expect that it will report two different readings. One measures the temperature inside the house and the other outside. A similar principle is found in the internal and external readings of a confidence meter.

We estimate our own confidence level on the basis of our inner feelings. We appraise the confidence level of others on their outer appearance. From my observations and discussions with students and adults, I find that significant discrepancies are commonplace between the two readings. Opinions of our own confidence levels are consistently lower than the estimates others make of our confidence level based on external appearances. On the average I believe the discrepancy range is approximately two to one. In other words, on a scale of zero to 100, external-confidence level estimates of 90 would find self-confidence level readings in the neighborhood of 45. External estimates of 50 would find personal reports in the general area of 25.

The intelligence quotient (IQ) is widely studied and discussed. Yet any study of the competency quotient (CQ) has been largely ignored. It is good news that our competency quotient seems more subject to improvement than the IQ.

In spite of what external appearances suggest about my confidence level, I am frequently ill at ease in face-to-face meetings with strangers. That can even be true with people I know well.

As a high school freshman I apparently appeared confident enough to be elected to the school's representative council. At that time, however, I'm convinced my true self-esteem varied from below average to inferior. If I recognized someone I knew walking toward me a block away, I felt uncomfortable enough to cross the street to avoid a personal encounter.

I had little understanding why my self-confidence level was so fragile—I assumed it was normal for me. I haven't yet managed to overcome all these feelings. At times I still request my wife to initiate the contact with persons we don't know well.

THE DIPPER AND THE BUCKET

*D*onald Clifton is president of Selection Research Associates. I concur with his statement that "we all need to help others fulfill their own potentiality." In his theory of "The Dipper and The Bucket," Clifton suggests that everyone has an invisible bucket that is always with them. "It determines how we feel about ourselves . . . and how we get along with people. A bucket can be filled by a lot of things that happen. When a person says 'Good morning' to you, recognizing you as a human being, your bucket is filled a little—even more if he calls you by name. If he compliments or affirms you for a job well done, the level in your bucket goes up still higher. There must be a million ways to raise or to lower the level in another's bucket."

Clifton tells of attending a formal banquet and inadvertently spilling a cup of hot coffee over the table. He felt like wanting to stop the world and get off. Then someone down the table called out, "You upset your coffee!" Clifton comments,

> I had made a mistake and knew it immediately. When he announced to the world, "You upset your coffee," he got his dipper in my bucket.
>
> Buckets are filled and buckets are emptied. When a person's bucket is empty, he is a very different person than when it is full. The story of our lives can be viewed as an interplay of the dipper and the bucket.
>
> You cannot tell from the outside how full a person's bucket is . . . or if it is empty. A person may

be wearing a smile (a pleasant mask) on his face but be hiding an empty bucket. And the person that has an empty bucket can get very touchy.

The next time someone is right about what is wrong with you, and you already know it, just say, "Hey, you have your dipper in my bucket!" Better yet, when you hear others dipping into somebody else, say "We're getting our dippers in his bucket. We ought to be filling his bucket instead of dipping." In doing this we experience the mysterious power of the dipper and the bucket.

OUR KNACK FOR SELF-KNOCKING

I know of two sisters. The older sister has not only been a faithful and supportive wife to a successful businessman, but she has raised three Christian children and been a foster parent to several others. In addition, she has been a loyal friend to needy persons in her community. She gives of herself and her time even at the expense of her health—but refuses to count the cost. Yet how does she evaluate herself and her contributions in relation to her sister? She tends to depreciate herself and claim her accomplishments are of lesser importance. So go many of the self-evaluations throughout most families—each person convinced that the life of another is more rewarding, more service-oriented.

A child raised as an orphan may believe she was of no importance to anyone. Years later that person may realize she really was loved by those who cared for her. But what was authentic for her as a child was what she actually felt at that time. If she *felt* unloved then that was true for her. Because of this, all parents and friends of children should strive consistently to convince each child both of a deep love from adults and of an everlasting love of God.

I knew of a high school girl who told her counselor that she often felt she had no right to live. After a number of discussions the student clarified the source of her feelings. Years ago she had overheard her dad comment that she "ought not have been born." A one-time careless statement can burden a child with lifelong feelings of rejection. Our

22

self-image often is distorted because we remember and tend to believe the put-downs, criticisms, and rebukes heard when we were young and unable to make a more mature self-evaluation.

There are persons who would like to get married but can't bring themselves to consider it because of low self-esteem. How could anyone seriously love them? Aware of their low self-evaluation, they can't believe that others could have a much higher appraisal. So there are attractive men and women who won't date. They are convinced no one would wish to become romantically involved with them. They have a persistent fear of being spurned. Any rejection would pour salt on old wounds and demolish their already feeble self-esteem.

We have a divine challenge lovingly to draw out suppressed abilities in those who need greater self-confidence. Meeting that need, however, doesn't come naturally. In fact, it's difficult for many of us to express our love for our own family and friends. Lloyd John Ogilvie speaks to this in his book, *When God First Thought of You.*

> Over the years, I have observed that the people who are able to infuse this precious, liberating experience of self-esteem in others are people who feel good about themselves. They feel special and help others to know they are special. But that's not easy for most people. They are more aware of their shortcomings and inadequacies than their strengths and abilities. The ledger of self-evaluation lists more liabilities than assets. Creative self-love is difficult for many of us, knowing all we do about ourselves. And there is never a shortage of fellow self-negators around to fortify our negative self-image. It's hard to be up for other people when you are down on yourself (Lloyd John Ogilvie, *When God First Thought of You.* Copyright © 1978, p. 122; used by permission of Word Books, Publisher, Waco, Texas.)[2]

In summarizing the problem of low self-confidence, we eventually realize that we can be our own worst enemies. Many of us are self-rejectors. Unfortunately, this encourages us to reject others. Yet growth in feelings of personal adequacy is possible when we are convinced of God's loving concern and acceptance. Peter emphasizes this fact when he writes,

> Once you were less than nothing; now you are God's own. Once you knew very little of God's kindness; now your very lives have been changed by it.
> (1 Peter 2:10, TLB)

We also can be of significant help in improving levels of self-esteem for others. What an inspiring opportunity for loving service!

3
Infirming with Words

Why then do you criticize your brother's actions,
why do you try to make him look small?
Romans 14:10a (Phillips)

My single most infirming event occurred in third grade, when my teacher handed back a paper and told me there was a mistake on it." A successful professional woman was sharing this story. Her voice wavered with emotion as she recounted her experience.

I was to find the mistake and correct it. When I couldn't find the error the teacher became incensed and accused me of being stubborn and arrogant. I was punished by missing every recess until I found and corrected my error. This went on for days before she gave in and showed me my mistake. I had used "there" instead of "their." To her this was probably just a minor frustration. To me at eight years? Well, I came to believe that I must really be stupid not to find an error my teacher thought was so obvious. The scenarios changed as I grew older, but similarities were found in them all—a significant other person in my life assigns a task which I can't complete either to my satisfaction or theirs. The lingering effects of such infirming seem unshakable.

UNREQUESTED ADVICE AS CRITICISM

How many times have we heard "Perhaps I shouldn't say this, but...," "I don't mean to criticize, but...," or the justification after criticizing, "I was *only* trying to help!"

Superiors can immobilize subordinates with continual fault-finding. Unless requested, advice contains a veiled criticism and sows seeds of inadequacy. We can incapacitate persons by unrequested advice as much as by a direct criticism.

Most of us are more sensitive to being infirmed than we realize. Unrequested criticism lowers our sense of importance, cripples our confidence, and calls forth resentments.

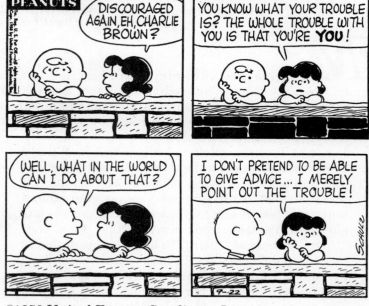

©1958 United Feature Syndicate, Inc.

Fritz Ridenour, author of *How to Be a Christian Without Being Religious,* offered some thoughts on verbal infirming in a TV interview. He identified the following communication pitfalls:

(a) jabbing or cutting comments that hurt.
(b) using the words "always" or "never" when talking about the conduct of others. Seldom are such conditions true, and their use is discouraging.
(c) using "double-meaning" words. Normally they will

be taken in the most negative way and the listener will feel put-down.

(d) jumping to conclusions. Assuming the other person is wrong before listening for all the facts.

(e) repeating lectures a family member has heard time and again. Not considering what you may have done under similar circumstances.

CHILDREN CAN'T FIGHT BACK

*I*nfirming by parents incapacitates children at an early age. It is difficult to overcome. Children want to like themselves, to have high self-esteem. But when parents belittle them, children feel demoralized. They become ashamed both of their failures and of themselves.

Adults who are insecure often put down children because they can't fight back. The children's eyes can betray their dejected feelings. "I'm a disappointment to my parents. No one likes me. Why was I ever born?"

Parents infirm children in many ways. One person remembers her mother's statement, "You weren't planned and you weren't wanted." How utterly crushing to be told that you were unwanted by the very person that brought you into the world! Another youngster had a father she admired. Normally he was a loving person. Yet on occasions he would say, "You are so dumb!" Her mother was usually supportive. Yet at times she would tag her daughter with, "You're just like me. We can't do anything." Fifty years later this person still feels handicapped in the area of self-confidence.

In his book, *The Strong and the Weak,* Paul Tournier tells of a person who was staying at a friend's house. He noticed how frequently the parents gave orders to their child. Later he counted the orders given in a two-hour period—a total of 120 orders. Forty-six were things he should do. Seventy-four were things he should not do![1] Such an avalanche of words can overwhelm a child's floundering self-confidence. Internal deafness can result. The child may learn to shut out statements of other persons the rest of his life.

Another child had a conviction that she was undesirable. When little, she wanted to sit on her mother's lap. The mother always said, "No, I can't hold you. You hurt my knees." Where else can a child find so much security as in her own mother's lap, leaning on her breast? What a distressing rebuff! Emotional infirming of young children may be a primary cause of emotional disorders in adult life.

PLEASE BE PLEASED WITH ME

A former president of the American Personnel and Guidance Association, Merle Ohlsen, shared this observation.

I have watched a fine Christian parent belittle a teenager in front of others. It was for things the youth shouldn't have done, but the parent's anger and need to satisfy revenge not only hurt the youngster, but reduced his will to change and not repeat the inappropriate behavior.

In *Irregular Persons,* Joyce Landorf tells of parents who never attended any of their daughter's swim meets. They ignored the fact that she broke all swimming records in most events her first year of high school. Later, as a senior, she became the secretary of both her class and the student body, but at no time did either parent acknowledge her accomplishments.

Reviewing this time in her life the daughter said, "I tried *so* hard to make my parents see that I was capable." When she won the title of Homecoming Queen her senior year, she recalled thinking, "*Now* they'll be proud of me!" But her mother's only comment was "I guess it pays to be cheap with the boys." Her mother would be fortunate if her low moral expectations did not become a self-fulfilling prophecy for her daughter. To avoid disabling their children, parents must be eternally vigilant, considering the lasting consequences of their words before they speak.

Thoughtless labeling by parents often results in self-fulfilling prophecies for their children. Call a youngster stupid and you make him less capable of living up to his potential. If a mother continually tells a pretty young girl that she is plain, the girl may develop such limited confidence that if a man looks at her very long she mistakes his admiration for disapproval. The mother may have made these comments to her daughter to keep her from becoming conceited. Or the mother may have worried that her daughter might outshine her own need for attention.

Children also can be ridicule victims of adults who need to build themselves up by putting others down. My wife's third grade instructor was teaching for the first time. Lois idolized her for a while. After a spelling test one day, the teacher wrote a misspelled word on the chalkboard. Before the whole class she laughed at the way Lois had spelled "curtain." Today Lois is a freelance writer. Words are her stock in trade. Yet when writing the word "curtain," the insecurity lingers and she still often needs to check the correct spelling in the dictionary.

From the time she was a child, a young woman had wanted to become a medical doctor. As a college student she had some difficulty with a demanding physics course. Her professor declared that anyone having trouble in a physics class, especially a girl, could never expect to get into medical school. Fortunately for the welfare of thousands of future patients, she refused to be devastated by his graceless and inaccurate judgment. Later she graduated from medical school and served as a medical missionary in Southeast Asia for five years. Today she is a successful pediatrician in the Midwest specializing in children's mental health.

How many potential servants of mankind have had their self-esteem blown away by inappropriate recommendations of misinformed or careless infirmers?

A *BRUISED BY TAUNTING AND TEASING*

*A*buse by taunting is not new. Matthew tells of people making fun of Jesus—mocking Him, jeering at Him, and taunting Him. These were forerunners of greater infirming acts to follow (Matthew 27:44).

According to medical specialists, laughter *with* others can help to reduce pain and cure a patient. On the other hand, laughter *at the expense of* another person can vary from being an embarrassment to an agonizing experience. Laughter, like teasing, can move a person into desperate loneliness, and at times into desperate action.

In *The Me Nobody Knows,* Stephen Joseph tells of the pain inflicted by name-calling. An overweight 13-year-old boy declared,

> Sometimes I feel as if everyone is looking at me so I walk a little faster or go out of my way so I won't see anyone I know. But then a little kid yells out, "The fat pig is going by!" I can't get out of that neighborhood fast enough.[2]

Many who are teased button their lips and suffer in silence. Others may seethe internally until they erupt in some unexpected reaction. Those who work with other people should consider whether physical abuse that is visible or emotional abuse that is invisible is more damaging.

Persistent teasing was a form of recreational activity in large families years ago, and the teasing trait can be passed through families from generation to generation. Once it is in the lineage, its practice is hard to discontinue.

My mother was raised on a large farm. She had six brothers with whom to compete before a baby sister was born. With no radio or television to absorb free time, teasing became a common expression of sibling rivalry. While there were other targets to harass, as the only girl my mother was for years the object of much teasing.

Similarly, teasing had a prominent place in my childhood home. I'm convinced it was never intended to hurt—just used as good-natured "fun." But the final evaluation of its "fun quality" has to be made by the teased, not the teasers. As the youngest member of the family, I often fell into the taunted class. I was asked repeatedly to pronounce the words "chrysanthemum" and "linoleum." Try as I would, I still mispronounced them, much to the entertainment of my family or guests in the home.

Years later I vowed not to laugh *at* anyone in our own family. Yet it was easy to slip into the familiar patterns I had experienced. On occasions I found myself teasing my wife. When this hurt her, I remembered my previous hurts and regretted my action immediately. Being continually cautious is the price I pay to break the intergenerational teasing chain. An old adage asks, "If you collected 10 cents for every kind word you speak to your spouse and paid five cents for every thoughtless word, would you be richer or poorer?"

G *SWAMPED BY COMPARISONS*

od makes no two individuals exactly alike. Each is unique. Each has an inherent right to be accepted as created. It deflates a child's self-concept when we say, "Why can't you be like your older brother or sister?" I felt inferior when my report cards were compared to my sister's. She had top grades all through school. There was pressure to be like my sister if I were to gain my parents' acceptance.

Comparisons hurt deeply and can damage self-esteem. Whether parents realize it or not, their expectations verbally discount one of their offspring. Comparisons with inanimate objects are less frequent, but they also can damage one's self-concept. Statements such as "You have a nose like a snow plow," or "You've got the shape of a sack of potatoes" are definitely infirming.

A lady I talked with in a retirement center shared this experience.

I remember that when I was younger, I couldn't dance. I wanted to learn so I went to Arthur Murray's Dance Studio. The instructor gave me two lessons. I had trouble mastering the steps. Finally he said, "Lady, you dance like a truck!" I haven't been dancing since. I may have been a little heavy on my feet, but that statement really put me down.

She felt unlovely. A careless tongue had steamrollered her self-esteem and killed her spirit to try again.

In Luther's Large Catechism he includes an explanation of the Eighth Commandment that is pertinent to this thinking.

This command, then, comprehends many great and good words exceptionally pleasing to God and bringing abundant blessings. . . .For there is nothing about a man nor in him that can do greater good or greater harm, in spiritual or in temporal matters, than this smallest and weakest of his members—the tongue.[3]

Evidently God is as interested as we are that we avoid infirming others or being infirmed by careless words. Rather our statements ought to be encouraging and positive and so fulfill His law of love.

The next chapter deals with the helpful ways we can use words to affirm, encourage, and appreciate others.

4
Affirming with Words

*Say only what is good and helpful
to those you are talking to,
and what will give them a blessing.*
Ephesians 4:29 (TLB)

I had a fourth grade teacher who did for me what God did for Jacob when He gave him a new name." Karen, a former work associate of mine, continued,

I was convinced I was "dumb." My teacher gave me a new name—"intelligent and curious." She moved me from the middle group to the top group in class. She paid close attention to me. If I fouled up, it wasn't "You didn't listen." Her attitude was, "Perhaps I didn't say this in a way that you understood." Her constant encouragement guided me in such a way that I early understood what was expected, sought help whenever needed, and felt confident I could achieve.

What tremendous influence teachers have—as well as parents and all of us when we respect and commend other persons. Sincere praise reassures individuals. It helps them neutralize doubts they have about themselves. If we decide to affirm and appreciate others, the time to start is today.

Every individual has some special talents, strengths, or abilities. When we observe and appreciate these strengths, we highlight them for the other person. Because our associates usually appear deceptively confident, we easily misjudge them as needing little affirmation. Their bold front appears invincible, but it usually is a mask of confidence. Beneath the front, one usually finds another self-critical, fearful person needing our affirmation.

33

JUST AS I AM

*A*friend showed me a letter he had received. I read the words, "God bless you for being you!" My friend smiled as he said, "This letter is most affirming, particularly because I know it contains no expectation that I be something I am not. It means to me that God also accepts my imperfect self and loves the me I really am."

Acceptance recognizes persons as they now are. Affirmation celebrates what they may yet become with God's help.

Gratitude is a special type of affirmation that pervaded Jesus' life on earth. Few of us, however, express thanks frequently enough to become effective at it. Generally we are pathetically ungrateful, not only toward our friends, our family members, and church servants but also toward God. This is in spite of God's goodness to us just as we are. "Out of the fullness of His grace He has blessed us all, giving us one blessing after another" (John 1:16, TEV). Thanksgiving is emphasized each November. Thanks-living is a year-round opportunity.

AFFIRMING IN SCHOOLS

*P*eople learn by their strengths and not by their weaknesses," stated a friend whose job for years was to supervise new teachers. She continued,

> I always chose positive points to comment on in the lesson so student teachers would gain self-confidence. They became convinced that I trusted them with the class because I showed complete confidence in their ability to be in control. When they had problems, I talked them over; I didn't take over. I tried to leave them with the feeling they were on their way to becoming excellent teachers.

Telling of the greatest teacher she ever had, Cynthia Parsons, Education Editor of the *Christian Science Monitor*, explained that one of her teachers treated students in a unique way. No matter how dumb a question was, the teacher always acted as if it were a good one. In fact, her goal was that students have more dignity after asking a question than before. She also challenged students by asking some in the room to help others with their problems.

"I remember one day," Parsons explained,

I heard a student who was the class "brain" ask the teacher how to work out a graph of an equation. She just turned to me with one of her choice smiles and asked if I'd mind showing him how cleverly I had done the problem. You know, I can *still* hear her saying the word "cleverly." That was the first time anyone had ever called me clever and I liked it! Her expectations gave me a new self-confidence—helped redirect my goals and my life.

Dick is an elementary school principal in Alaska who prompts parents with a special challenge. "Try to catch your child being good 10 times each day." He finds this practice beneficial, since most parents are quick to find the wrongs but slow to praise children for good behavior.

Dick also inaugurated another program to increase pupil self-esteem. He asks each substitute teacher to complete a report giving names of any students who were particularly helpful. Not only are these students recognized in front of the class, but the principal phones the parents to share the positive report of their child's thoughtful assistance.

J. Wesley Sullivan is Chairman of the Editorial Board of one of Oregon's major newspapers. He states that his first year in high school affected his whole life.

My freshman English teacher was Mrs. Blanche Thurston, one of the finest teachers I have known. One day she had me read an essay I had written to the class. Later she talked with me about it. Her evaluation concluded with, "Wes, you can write! I admired her so much—I had so much confidence in her I just had to believe her. So I started to write. I joined the school literary club and worked on the school paper. I had set my course, at age fourteen, into one of the most interesting fields of endeavor I could ever hope to enter. I will always be grateful there was a Mrs. Thurston who, at the right time, had sincere words of encouragement and praise for me. What a difference one positive person can make in a youth's life!

Human nature seems to take persons for granted.

Expressing gratitude is a neglected courtesy as the following letter illustrates. "My dear Willie . . . I can't tell you how much your note meant to me." Mrs. A. B. Wendt was replying to a letter from one of her former students.

> I am in my eighties, living alone, in a small room, cooking my own meals, lonely and like the last leaf of fall lingering behind. . . . You will be interested to know that I taught school for fifty years and yours is the first note of appreciation I ever received. It came on a blue, cold morning and it cheered me as nothing has in many years.

How many lonely Mrs. Wendts are there in our world? How many could still be affirmed, cheered, and their self-esteem boosted if those who feel appreciative would write a note of affirmation?

PUT YOUR AFFIRMATIONS IN WRITING

A written note of appreciation does take more time than saying "thank you." But written notes often are more supportive and nourishing. They may be shared with family members and close friends. They may be read over and over again when one's self-esteem needs a boost. A long distance between friends is no barrier to written words of praise.

In recent years, I have combined some of my "thank yous" with a celebration of the Thanksgiving season. Starting November 1, I set a goal of writing at least one appreciation note a day. My dateline becomes "Thanksgiving 19——." The notes are addressed to family members, relatives, employees, pastors, doctors, friends, or to organizations that have served faithfully and well. The range of possibilities is unlimited. A sincere feeling of appreciation is the only requirement. I mail the notes early Thanksgiving week and feel pleased when they are on their way.

During the past 10 years I have led several hundred management seminars for business, professional, and industrial organizations. In these I stress the close relationship between positive morale and expressions of praise or appreciation. After one seminar a lay church administrator wrote:

I have made a resolution to write a note each week during the next year to someone who has been an inspiration to me. When next year rolls around and I reflect on the fifty-two notes I have written—who knows—maybe I'll extend it to two years.

I contacted this woman a year later to learn what happened. She had written at least half the notes intended. She explained that almost *all* of the people responded in one way or another.

Many people approached me with tears in their eyes after they received a note—especially older people. They couldn't quite believe that *they* had made a contribution to my life. With many, a deeper and closer friendship has developed. My notes seemed to open doors and our friendship grew.

She also commented,

The experience made a couple of lasting impressions on my thinking: (a) People need to feel worthwhile. It nourishes them to hear that they have made some contribution for good in the lives of others. (b) Praise has a profound effect when it is written. It takes more effort to compose a note or a letter. But the person receiving it can read it again and again and enjoy the recognition for an indefinite period of time.

There is an additional effective way to express appreciation. I try to follow the advice, "If you don't like what I do, tell me. If you like what I do, tell my boss."

When my wife was admitted to the hospital for surgery, I was impressed by the caring and thorough manner in which the admitting clerk handled her duties. Knowing what a sensitive position that is, I felt a letter of commendation was in order. I addressed my note to the administrator of the hospital rather than to the admitting clerk. Several weeks later, I received a letter from the admitting clerk. She wrote that she appreciated my note to the administrator. She continued by writing,

What you don't know is that my husband is an invalid in a wheelchair, I am the sole support of the family, I have been on the house cleaning crew for years and just recently had an opportunity for promotion to the admitting desk.

Had I addressed the appreciation note to her, she could not have routed it up the organization. Since it entered at the top, however, each of her superiors could also enjoy the good news!

Another time when time I was driving on the freeway, a car from the opposite direction sideswiped the center concrete divider several times. If the divider had not been there, I might have been injured or killed in a head-on collision. Following this incident, I wrote to the State Highway Commission, told of the events, and expressed appreciation for the protection offered by the concrete dividers. A Mr. Versteeg replied that he receives many letters of criticism and complaint each year. My letter was one of the first to affirm their safety efforts. The only way the highway department employees know that accidents have been avoided is when they observe black tire marks on the sides of the dividers. He added that he had routed my letter to those departments responsible for design, installation, and maintenance of these safety features.

When we commend, we generate feelings of self-esteem and dignity in those we praise. It is one way we have of sharing God's love. Ben Franklin said, "As we must account for every idle word, so we must for every idle silence." Yet many of us seem tongue-tied when it comes to the ministry of encouragement. Silence is not always golden. Words of sincere praise may be all that keep some discouraged soul afloat.

A grandfather shared a beautiful affirming letter from his 19-year-old grandson. For a moment, picture yourself in this grandfather's situation. You are terminally ill—and you now receive what may be one of your life's most supportive communications.

> Dear Grandpa,
>
> Hello, Grandpa! I must be honest that this is a difficult letter to write, but I trust that God will make real to you "the hope which lies within us . . . ," and the deep appreciation and admiration I hold for you. . . .
>
> Grandpa, I sincerely want to thank you for the Godly example that you've been to me, as long as I've known you. Your life has brought forth "fruit" which has really made an impact on my life, and I

know it will continue to make an impact on others through me. Thank you for being a good listener, and for taking time to share parts of your life with me.

I love you, Grandpa, and I rejoice that we *both* are heirs of the Father, and Jesus Christ. We have an inheritance beyond human understanding. Only those who have truly seen the Father's goodness can begin to comprehend the *joy* of entering God's kingdom!

Grandpa, I cherish you, and I know that the present circumstances may seem very depressing, but our God has all things in control, and He can be trusted—hard as it is at times!

Thank you, Grandpa, for who you are, and what you've been to me—a *grand* father. Can we get together and talk when I get to heaven? I'd love to spend more time with you!!!

Your grandson,

I have no doubts that the grandfather was well pleased with his grandson. There are some interesting similarities in this situation to God's notable affirmation, "You are my own dear Son, I am well pleased with you" (Mark 1:11, TEV).

How many life-enriching affirmations have we thought of sharing with others but never completed because of our excuse, "I don't know what to say." A grandson with God's help has shown us the way. What a positive influence we can have in the lives of others if we will follow his example!

5
Infirming unto the Third and Fourth Generation

*There is no character, howsoever good
and fine, but it can be destroyed
by ridicule, howsoever poor and witless.*
Mark Twain

THE INFIRMING CYCLE

Many parents recreate with their children the style in which they previously were raised. If abused when young, parents have a predisposition to abuse their children who then will feel more rejected than respected.

Children of abusing parents feel lonely. They also feel confused, inadequate, and unloved. Unless there is an understanding of how infirming cycles work and a concerted effort to break the cycle, abusing parents will continue to beget abusing parents.

One subtle characteristic of the abusing parent is found in many positive, "healthy" families. This is the quality of making excessive and premature demands on children. Parents who feel they did not succeed as children can fall into a pattern of placing perfectionist demands on their offspring. This can result in unconscious pressures to excel, EXCEL, *EXCEL!* The child not attracted to or unable to excel in his parents' special interest will disappoint both the parents and himself. This results in feelings of guilt and shame which precede becoming a dropout from the family activity, from those things the parents hold dear, or even from society. While small, a child is still a compliant prisoner in his family environment. When older, the more he

41

feels pushed into uninteresting activities, the greater the distance from home he achieves when breaking away.

A friend who states that his father never affirmed him adds,

> I think I have been guilty of putting down my own children at times. I am conscious it has hurt them deeply, though they rarely say so. I called my son's behavior "boorish" in public on one occasion, and he has never forgotten it. He has mentioned it a number of times. It hurt him more than I knew.

I discussed affirming and infirming behavior with residents of several retirement centers. One man cited how he was the third boy in his family. He remembers feeling unwanted by his two brothers. Very often he recalls them saying to him, "No, we don't want you along." Seventy years later he still dreams about his two brothers saying, "We don't want you along!" Rejection has tenacious staying power inside an individual.

An oriental lady in one retirement center commented that her parents were "basement people."

> At least in my home it was a custom not to praise anyone. They always tried to drag you down—very negative—that's how it was with me anyway. My father always said I was very ugly. More recently I have tried to practice positive thinking, but I am still fighting the negative feelings I had about myself as a little girl. He used to say, "It's no use for you to go to school, 'cause you're a dummy." So I tried to raise my children with a positive rather than a negative attitude, but it was difficult to shut out the way I had been raised.

DON BARTLETTE, RETARDED CHILD TO PH.D.

Don Bartlette was born in North Dakotapoor, handicapped, and an American Indian. He had only half a nose, no upper lip, and a cleft palate. As a child he never could speak understandably. Today he holds an earned Doctor of Philosophy degree.

Don's early experiences affected his entire life. "My

father wanted me to be like him—a big man, a brave man—not a handicapped child who couldn't even speak." It was bad enough to be handicapped, to be Indian, to be poor. "What really hurt was being unwanted by my own father."

The local school board insisted he enroll in school when he was nine years old. Don suffered rejection, humiliation, and abuse as a result. Children gathered around him and called out, "Flat nose, flat nose, you can't talk" or "Donald Duck, say quack, quack." At other times he was infirmed with names like "Retard," Smelly Injun," or "Half-breed harelip."

Adults should know better, but some were scarcely more accepting. Don heard a teacher say, "Why did the principal put him in my room?" Later he heard the second grade teacher say, "I don't want him in my class." So she arranged for his social promotion to the third grade. Of those years Don summarized, "I didn't want people laughing at me! I was aching for someone to touch my life, to accept me, to love me, to help me learn to talk!"

Several years later someone completely changed Don's life. She was a well-educated woman in a beautiful home who asked Don's grandmother to bring him to her.

She asked me to wash her automobile. I had never done that—I didn't even know that water could come out of a faucet. But she was willing to come into my foreign world, the world of the handicapped, even though she could not understand me at all when I tried to talk. But she did come into my lonely life. For the first time in my life I felt a hand gently touch mine. I cannot describe that feeling adequately enough when she touched my hand and put it over the faucet. She came back into my world again when she took my hand and showed me how to wash the automobile.

She taught me more too. I had never had a positive thought about anyone. This white woman's acceptance of me, just as I was, helped me start to purge myself of hate. Later I even began to learn to speak. The white woman put her fingers in my mouth to move my tongue. Can you imagine her putting her fingers in the mouth of a "retarded" Indian?

Emotional damage such as Don experienced is more easily recognized in severe situations. But any of us can infirm others in so many subtle ways. It is possible to chip away at a person's self-esteem with such small but persistent blows that an individual can be slowly but surely destroyed. Indirect attacks of jealousy, hostility, and hate can be more destructive than a direct confrontation.

As a nationally known speaker, Don Bartlette now pleads the case for all handicapped persons. "Think of them first as individuals who hurt, who want to know love, and who need to be encouraged and affirmed."

It is important to remember that what happens to a child will affect that person as long as he or she lives. If we will take the risk of reaching out in love as the white woman did to Don and touch the person who is hurting, we can share God's love and make a priceless contribution to one of His creatures.

A GENERATION TO GENERATION INFIRMING

A major problem in society today is a feeling of low self-esteem experienced by the elderly. Many senior citizens report they feel like "nobodies." A combination of problems may be the cause—the loss of loved ones, a move to strange surroundings, loss of status, and loneliness. Family members may be far away or they may be as thoughtless about writing or visiting the elderly. The effects are the same. Some elderly say, "To be unseen and unheard is devastating." In reality they suffer a type of divorce if they are ignored by negligent family members.

Studies have shown that children prefer negative attention to feeling ignored. Could the same situation be true for the elderly? Is there any cause and effect relationship between feelings of being ignored and the recent increase in the arrest rate age? Some unidentified factors must account for the 46 percent increase in arrest records of elderly persons.

Physical abuse is fairly common today. The results are obvious. Bruises or broken bones can't be concealed. Though abused feelings are invisible, the resulting emotional scars are deeper and longer lasting. Infirming practices can be so ingrained they are like an inherited characteristic. The transforming love of God through Christ, however, can break the infirming link between generations.

A leader in state government told me of infirming traits in his family which he has been able to identify through three generations.

"It seems to me," he explained, "that psychological infirming tendencies are passed from one generation to another in much the same way that physically abused children tend to become child abusers when they are adults." He is convinced the cycle is hard to break unless family members experience the renewing and healing power of God's love. He continued:

I didn't become an infirmer because of any direct abuse from Dad. His attacks were directed either at himself or at the one he loved most, his wife. No matter how perfect a family meal or how special it might have been, seldom could he give a compliment to my mom. And as hard as they worked in their business over the years, nothing was ever quite enough as my dad viewed it. And most of the time he was nearly as hard on himself as he was on Mom. It seemed to me that if he had been able to accept himself and God's forgiving love, he would not have needed to ridicule and put down others the way he did.

I vowed I would never follow or duplicate his example. Yet it showed its influence in our marriage, particularly through the first ten years. I found myself putting my wife down just as my dad had done to my mother. More frustrating yet, we observed our son in the early years of his marriage, and the same patterns tended to emerge. Fortunately, my wife and I reached a point some years ago where we could begin to talk about it—but oh, how deep the scars were that I hardly knew existed! It has been only in recent years that we've been able to discuss and share these heartaches of our marriage without both of us to some extent coming apart.

Because we were fortunate enough to spot some

of these problems, we decided to discuss them with our kids early in their marriage. We hoped they could become aware of their "inheritance" and discontinue some of the infirming patterns now affecting their lives. I think it has been helpful. Now they are aware of some of their legacies going back as far as their grandfather. Yet, if it weren't for the Lord's love working in our lives, it's probable the infirming cycle of destructive behavior would continue to recur in future generations.

How essential it is to understand that the patterns we use to mold those we love tend to be a replication of patterns that were used to mold our behavior. And how relevant, then, is Paul's caution when he says, "Don't let the world squeeze you into its mold, but let God remold your minds from within, so that you may prove in practice that the plan of God is good for you . . . and moves toward the goal of true maturity" (Rom. 12:1-2, Phillips).

6
Infirming with Actions

*What you do speaks so loudly
I can't hear what you say.*
Anonymous

Although children need loving discipline, they can be handicapped by authoritarian attitudes. Some parents may unknowingly be gaining vengeance for the rigid type of punishment they received in childhood. I had to resist letting snap judgments and quick anger control my disciplining actions with our children.

Physical child abuse is receiving more attention from the media and legislative bodies. Nationally, the reported incidence of child abuse rose 68 percent between 1981 and 1982. The reports of child abuse in Oregon increased 3,900 percent between 1971 and 1982—from 86 to 3,369 cases. Yet I believe more children are emotionally abused by parents than are physically abused.

ATTITUDES, THE MAINSPRINGS TO ACTION

Children are very vulnerable to negative adult attitudes. Even though children are given clothing, home, education, and gifts, parental attitudes can still deny the tenderness and love for which a child yearns. Most children would give up physical gifts to feel assured of the faithful love of their parents. Hurt and hostility arise within the child who senses rejection by his parents. The resulting personality problems often impair a later capacity for effective interpersonal relationships.

47

Adults can be infirmed in much the same way. A college dean was making a major address before a group of distinguished scientists. Later he remarked to me that "a noted neurologist looked only at the papers in front of him and never once bothered looking at me as the speaker." That left him to guess whether the person was sleepy, uninterested, bored, or in total disagreement with his presentation. The speaker felt infirmed.

An attitude that stifles mutual understanding can do serious harm to marital relationships. An adult's cruel laughter at a marriage partner is psychologically abusive. To make fun of a spouse's needs or hobbies unveils a mocking attitude that sabotages the other person's self-esteem.

More damage is done by laughing *at* other persons than we realize. Scornful laughter results in more than embarrassment—it may cause heartbreak and create hate. I can't conceive of a loving heavenly Father laughing at me. So if earthly parents laugh at my awkwardness, my appearance, or my life-goals, the scorn will cut much deeper than they realize. Mockery of this type may infirm some children and youth for life.

We often ignore or rationalize Jesus' words, "Judge not that you be not judged" (Matt. 7:1). I want to interpret this commandment to mean, "Judge not unjustly. . . ." This lets me off the hook, as all *my* judgments are carefully reasoned out to be for another person's good—not snap judgments like others make. How deceptive such self-justification can be! Jesus did not deny there was a mote in my neighbor's eye. But He still says "Judge not." What a loss God must suffer since I feel so well qualified to help Him judge others! But He still says to me, "Judge not, Ken. Leave that to Me." Eventually I realize that judging others creates unbridgeable gulfs. It prevents the openness and acceptance necessary to relate to other individuals. Rather than freeing persons from their faults, my judgment encourages the denial or justification of their faults. That is more harmful than helpful.

Jesus gave the classic response to man's obsession for judging. The scribes and the Pharisees were planning to trap Him with the question about stoning the woman who had been caught in adultery. He quietly advised them that the person who was faultless should cast the first stone. What appropriate reproof for today's world!

A judgmental attitude leads to many infirming acts. The injustice is that I judge myself by my intentions, not by my actions. At the same time I judge others by their actions, not by their intentions. As one wit commented, "What I like most about myself is that I'm so understanding when I do something wrong." Such a double standard is inconsistent with Christ's admonition to love my neighbor as myself.

G *LABELS CONCEAL THE AUTHENTIC PERSON*

*G*ardening of the categories causes us to lose sight of individuals and their needs. We cover persons with labels such as priest, cashier, diplomat, military officer, receptionist, senator, or flight attendant. We have allowed the personage or the title to eclipse the person when we see someone functioning in a characteristic capacity but fail to notice the individual person who is actually performing the function.

When we accentuate the personage and ignore the person, we do damage to an individual's self-esteem. For example, we infirm an individual when we say: "We have an appendectomy in room 128," "There's a grievant in the outer office waiting to see you," "Social Security #540-07-5516 is holding on line three," or "I'm sending a troublemaker to the principal's office." We paste general labels on specific personalities. We shroud their individuality in the process.

Children get two major messages in our society. First, they need to be physically attractive, and, second, they should learn easily in school. The average adult gives special attention to the attractive child. Observing this, the child with a face full of pimples, with big feet, a hooked nose, crowded teeth, or prominent ears soon gets the feeling he or she is worth less than others. The child suffers extra pain when someone says, "You don't have any shape," "You're the tallest girl in the class," or "How come you're so awkward?" One significant cause of teenage suicide today is the conviction that "I'm ugly." Youth equate being physically unattractive with being unwanted and unloved both by peers and by adults.

Children are also quick to conclude that if they really want adult approval, they must succeed in school. Most parents' minimum standard requires that their child's performance be at least "above average."

One January when I was a high school principal, a distraught mother pushed her way into my office. Her problem was that her daughter's grades were below the family expectations. I studied her daughter's academic history and her standardized test scores before conferring with her counselor. Our conclusion was that the student already was doing as well as anyone had a right to expect. After a lengthy discussion, the concerned mother understood our interpretation of her daughter's learning potential. Yet she found it impossible to accept the evaluation. She summarized her defiance and discomfort with, "Well, I might be able to accept the fact that my daughter is average in learning ability, but I will never be able to accept that she is below average!"

Difficult as it is for parents to accept, "below average" is every bit as normal as "above average." This is true whether we consider a youth's height, weight, rate of growth, running speed, musical ability, or academic grades. Parental desires and pressures for every child to be academically above average are not only unrealistic, but can be unloving. Simple statistics reveal that about half of all students in our nation always will be below average scholastically. How rejected and worthless do we cause these children to feel both at school and at home?

On another occasion a concerned father came to my office to see what more he could do to help his son improve his high school grades. The father was unhappy with his son's C's, D's, and occasional F's. He was fully convinced that his son could earn A's and B's if he would only work harder. The father related to me how he required his son to sit at the kitchen table every evening and study. If his son fell asleep over his homework, the dad said with some smugness that he would knock his son off the chair, after which his son would pick himself up and start studying again.

Sensing that his comment had surprised me, the father quickly added that he also used positive psychology. More than anything else his son wanted a horse. So the father had promised to buy a saddle for him when he earned grades of B and C. And he promised to get a horse for him when he had earned grades of A and B.

Knowing of his son's low learning ability, I explained as considerately as possible that while his son undoubtedly was above averaage in a number of other areas, *academically* he happened to be below average—along with half of the other fine citizens in our nation. After some silence, the father remarked with new insight, "I guess my son will never ride his own horse according to my plan, will he?"

Every one of us is below average in some of life's activities. For example, I am below average in auto repairing, violin playing, computer knowledge, fly fishing, plumbing, weaving, nuclear physics, and oil painting to mention a few. I try, therefore, to look on everyone I meet as my superior in some way. I try to discover, celebrate, and praise the unique gifts and abilities in each of God's creatures. It is noteworthy to realize that by increasing pressures on children to excel in areas where they are not gifted, we infirm them and tarnish their self-esteem.

Adults want the best for and from their children. We want them to perform well. So we fall into the trap of comparing unique individuals to whom God has given extremely different talents. Then we depreciate some of them as "worth less" when we brand them "below average." Yet they are no less precious in the eyes of their Creator and in no way deserve to suffer rejection by parents, peers, educators, or relatives. All youth should realize that they have special and unique God-given talents. They need to understand that they don't have to meet man-made prerequisites to be acceptable to God. How different our world could be if the energy expended for fault-finding was used for 'talent-scouting' in our children, spouse, friends and acquaintances! One person has the possibility of beginning a chain reaction of praise and affirmation in a home, at work, in the neighborhood, at church. That is good news!

SQUARE PEGS AND ROUND HOLES

A slapdash method of assigning persons to organizational responsibilities can be infirming. We lower the self-esteem of others through our zeal to keep vacancies filled regardless of the "fit" of the new appointee. We often stuff triangular persons into round holes and force oblong persons into square holes. This lack of sensitivity to the unique talents of each person is a common hazard that inflicts unrealistic role expectations on individuals with little or no consideration of what they wish to do or can do well.

Congregations are often careless in this area. Mis-assignments are common simply because "we want to fill a committee vacancy promptly." We are cautious about giving unrealistic assignments to the obviously handicapped, such as the blind. Yet we ask some individuals to accept incompatible responsibilities with little attention to the person's interests and abilities. Carelessness in making appropriate assignments can result in both the person's self-esteem and God's work suffering.

*I*NFIRMING THROUGH SILENCE

I was visiting in the office of a school district maintenance supervisor. He reported how he felt ignored and infirmed by the organization. "This has got to be one of the loneliest, unappreciated, and difficult jobs around," he remarked. "It's only at the end of the month when a piece of paper comes with my name on it that I feel anyone knows I'm here—and the check is probably put out by a computer!"

In conversations with county jail inmates I find they sense a feeling of neglect; there also is a conviction of abandonment, often by their own family. One inmate declared, "I quit looking for mail a long time ago. Nobody's visiting and nobody's writing."

A lady in a retirement home told of her childhood on a California farm. Her dad had 80 acres of uncleared stump land. She commented,

I had to be his helper and I worked very hard. But he ignored all I did—never showed any appreciation. Gradually I became convinced he didn't love me. He must have wanted me just for my labor, and did I work hard! I pulled one end of a cross-cut saw with my dad. I chopped trees and piled wood and stacked hay. I worked harder than any girl should, and the conviction grew that my dad didn't love me. Being unloved became a reality for me.

One day a neighbor came by and dad bragged about me. He said that I worked like a trooper all day. The next day I worked twice as hard, but he still ignored me and my work. He *never* did affirm me directly in any way.

Ignoring others confirms what they sense as our disregard of them. Congregational cliques can undermine the love and fellowship that current members or new arrivals seek in church organizations. Enjoying favorite friends can blind us to lonely members or to visitors who long not to be treated as strangers.

If visitors spoke their true feelings to us we might hear them say, "Please, someone let me know that I am seen and acceptable here, that I am worth talking to. But for God's sake, don't just leave me all by myself. You preach that God is love, but no one here seems to care!" Doc Streator put it all in a few words when he said, "Neglect is eloquent rejection."

7
Affirming with Actions

*Do not withhold good from those to whom
it is due, when it is in your power to do it.*
Proverbs 3:27

*T*he animal kingdom can teach human beings some
valuable lessons according to Leo Bustad, Dean Emeritus of
Veterinary Medicine at Washington State University. He
reports that when raising pups, the mother dog gives a ratio
of nine gentlings to one growl or nip. Man in his affirming
versus infirming efforts appears less humane than his best
friend, the dog!

I find it instinctive to criticize, judge, or depreciate
others. Yet those of us who know God's love should be the
pacesetters when it comes to recognition and praise.

THE STIMULUS OF HIGH EXPECTATIONS

*P*ersons we treat like "A" students usually act like "A"
students. What we expect of others and the way we treat
them affects their performance and their attitude toward
themselves.

When I was high school principal, our students occasionally would sponsor a "Grubby Day" and at other
times a "Dress-up Day." Their behavior was predictable on
each occasion. They sensed the way they were *expected* to
act in each situation. And they followed through with
behavior fitting each event. There were faculty complaints
about student conduct on "Grubby Day," for young people
were acting in a sloppy manner. When "Dress-up Day"

arrived, we had a school of surprisingly mature young men and women. They conducted themselves in a manner that would have been a compliment to any segment of society. When much is expected, individuals tend to rise to the anticipated conduct level.

As a principal I had to write evaluations of all staff members. When a teacher was good to outstanding, I celebrated the fact by preparing an excellent, affirming report. On more than one occasion a teacher would ask, "Is that really me?" I responded that my evaluation simply mirrored the good qualities and commendable teaching observed. Often the teacher's reply was, "Well, I don't know if that is me now, but I'm certainly going to try to become that person!"

An interesting experiment revealed how individuals are affected by expectations. Two Headstart teachers were selected who were as equal as possible in potential and in practice. Then pupils were carefully tested, and two classes were formed that were as similar as possible in background and learning potential. Next the principal talked with each teacher alone. He told the first teacher how fortunate she was. "You have a class of high potential pupils this year! Just don't stand in their way. They're racers and ready to run." The second teacher was told, "I'm sorry about your pupils this year. But you can't expect top pupils every year. Just do the best you can. We'll be understanding regardless of the results." At the end of the year the two classes were tested again. The first class was significantly ahead of the second. The major differentiating factor appeared to be each teacher's expectations.

A former doctoral student of mine was inspired in his new administrative position. Roger's supervisor called him in to discuss a project requiring original work. My friend expected several people to be involved in a large project of that size. Then he learned that he alone would be responsible for the undertaking.

I found it exciting, yet hard to believe that the supervisor thought I was capable of providing leadership for such a responsibility. My boss's actions spoke of his confidence in my abilities by entrusting the entire project to me. The feeling I had is hard to describe.

As a beginning, untested administrator Roger reacted with a strong sense of responsibility. He worked enthusiastically. When finished with the assignment he had a feeling of accomplishment. Because of the experience he declared, "I now have a new conviction of self-confidence."

Jesus didn't search for proven experience when selecting his apostles. His actions expressed confidence in an assorted collection of fishermen, tax collectors, a carpenter, and others who became the nucleus of a worldwide community of believers. Who else would have seen the potential to build a kingdom on these unlikely candidates? And who would have seen in an enemy the potential of becoming the greatest apostle, Paul?

We too have opportunities to challenge inexperienced individuals to develop new skills. If our confidence convinces them that they have the potential, they often will meet or exceed our expectations. Several studies have concluded that high expectations tend to stimulate their own fulfillment. To the degree that we set low expectations for others, we hinder the growth God would have us foster in their lives. Paul's guideline for confidence in others is expressed in 2 Corinthians 7:16 where he says, "I rejoice therefore that I have confidence in you in all things" (KJV).

GIFTS EXPRESS LOVE

I was hospitalized with pneumonia at the age of 10. My family and a few friends visited me. While convalescing at home, I also was visited by a young couple from our church. Al and Myrtle drove from the other side of town just to call on me! And they brought a gift—a large black book with gold lettering on the cover. I still remember the title, *Young Fu of the Upper Yangtze*. More meaningful than the visit or the book was the evidence of their caring about me, their love for a very ordinary young child. They gave a solid boost to my self-esteem. I have never forgotten their special act of love.

Often we let similar opportunities slip away with our culture's number one alibi, "I am too busy right now." Yet we always have time for those things we put first. The hungering for gifts isn't so much a desire for gratification as it is a proof of affection. A person's need to be loved is limitless. So the real meaning of gifts is in the love they express.

We have a supreme example for giving in our heavenly Father. Proof of His love is the incomparable gift of His Son, plus complete forgiveness of sins, plus full acceptance of us just as we are. Such abundant gifts of affirming love are the solid foundation for a Christian's sense of dignity and feelings of self-worth.

TRUST AND SELF-ESTEEM

*T*rust is basic to self-esteem. If someone gives me a responsibility but then pulls it back at the slightest hint of difficulty, the level of trust expressed is not high. At that point I feel inadequate and resentful.

The trusting leader will talk things over, not take things over. Coaching from the sidelines is helpful. Conversely, grabbing the ball and saying, "Here, let a pro handle that" demonstrates a real lack of trust.

Jesus seldom spoke directly to the topic of praise or the topic of trust in the gospels. However, Doc Streator points out that

> Speaking silently through His actions as He did so effectively, Jesus goes far beyond not criticizing individuals. And this in spite of the fact that He knows about all our faults. In one beautiful moment we realize that His message of unqualified love illuminates His gracious trust in each of us. In effect Jesus says to you and to me, "You are worthy of My life." He gives His life so we can be truly alive. We are affirmed by God Himself. This is an affirmation of unwarranted trust in its highest form!

TALKING AND TOUCHING

*T*he human voice can be very affirming to others. Our family lived in the Rhine Valley of Germany for a year. While there, my wife, Lois, volunteered to help at a home for babies and their unwed mothers.

On her first visit, she was ushered into the director's office. A pleasant, blonde woman greeted her but couldn't offer her a place to sit. The small office was too full. It held the usual desk, work table, and filing cabinets. The unexpected piece of furniture that caught Lois's attention, however, was a baby basket. She looked down at a peacefully sleeping infant.

Noticing her surprise, the director said, "I always keep one or two babies in the office. This way the child can hear a human voice and feel more loved and secure." She reached for the baby and placed her in Lois's arms.

This is little Annette. I hold her often in the office. I also instruct my nurses to pick up every infant in the nursery several times a day to pat the child's back, talk to it, and give it some love. Our babies need more than food and dry diapers!

Touching is an act of affirmation. Listen to the report of an acquaintance who had lost her husband. She shared the following experience.

I was having lunch with a friend who was unaware of the recent death in our family. On learning of it, she reached across the table, took my hand, and held it for 5 to 10 minutes. She was normally a very busy person, but now her actions emphasized that she would sit in silence with me for eternity, were that helpful. It was like we were taking "time out of time."

Another woman told how, at the time of a death in the family, the most meaningful communication came to her in the form of hugs, pats on the shoulder, and squeezes of her hand. She added that while people may not know what to say, their hands, arms, faces, and eyes can express everything they find difficult to put into words.

THE GIFT OF TIME

*T*ime also is an affirming gift. A dear friend recently lost her hearing and entered the world of complete silence. She wrote to me:

A letter from a friend that I would not expect to write, saying nice things about me, bolstered my ego which really needed shoring up. I plan to reread this letter whenever things look bleak again. Such communications are a plus—because someone had taken the *time* to write to me.

Helping others grow in self-acceptance takes time. Two of my friends work with the socially maladjusted and learning-disabled students in the public schools. One of them, a principal, says that such youth have been crippled emotionally by previous infirming experiences. The youth come to expect that their performance will not meet their teachers' standards. Unless the disadvantaged have some successful affirming experiences in their lives, even remedial programs cannot succeed.

A principal tells of Jerry, who appeared for school a month and a half late one year. His parents were uneasy about enrolling him because of a long history of negative school experiences. Jerry threw a temper tantrum when his parents said they were going to leave him at school. Once enrolled he was almost totally uncooperative and rude. He dressed sloppily and left his hair uncombed.

Jerry was terrified at the thought of going to the cafeteria among hundreds of students to whom he was a stranger. Two students volunteered to bring his lunch to the Special Services office. A perceptive counselor video-taped interview sessions with Jerry and played them back to him. Jerry was tremendously surprised at what he saw. He sputtered out that he could not believe it was himself whom he was really watching. At this point miraculous changes began to occur. What unfolded was a young man embarrassed by his appearance and actions, wishing his peers would respect him, and longing for a better relationship with his father. Here was a young man changed by caring students and a counselor who gave the gift of extra time.

In discussion sessions with prison inmates I found them in universal agreement on the importance of visits. If a prisoner is from a different part of the nation, and some local person, a complete stranger, takes time for a visit, the inmate *knows* that that individual cares. Such calls usually have no overtones of critical judgment. In this positive relationship, the prisoner need not justify himself or his present condition. The visitor already has accepted the inmate just as he is.

Unfortunately, some friends and relatives give only conditional love. They will accept the prisoner *if* he straightens out and does things their way. But strangers who give of their time are accepting a person for what he can become. One prisoner commented, "Such a visit, especially from someone I don't know, keeps my attitude twice as strong in there. It changes my outlook on life once I'm convinced somebody has taken the time to care about me as an individual."

In one of Russia's largest churches in Zgorsk, the bishop addresses each of the thousands of communicants by their Christian name when serving them the Sacrament. What a personal manifestation of God's caring! What a contrast to the anonymity of a depersonalized secular society in which they live and work!

Recognizing individuals and calling them by name is an evidence of their worth—a boost to self-worth. Picture mentally where you spend your time each day. Visualize the paths your feet make as you move throughout your daily "territory." Which persons at work or in your neighborhood are you affirming with your presence? Do you call them by name, offer a warm greeting, share a smile? Which neighbors or co-workers are you unintentionally avoiding? Do you intend that they feel ignored, infirmed, and worth less?

In his book, *Ask Me to Dance,* Bruce Larson tells of Birch Foraker, who was president of the Bell Telephone Company in New York City.

When going to or from the theater fully dressed in his evening clothes, he would leave his companions and climb down into a manhole in the middle of the street. Why? Because there were men down there doing some emergency telephone work and he wished to encourage them. He wanted them to know he appreciated their work on a blustery winter's night.[1]

His employees felt affirmed by his thoughtfulness and presence. We can't all go down into manholes. Yet we often overlook other affirming opportunities right at our feet.

Individuals also can know of your love for them through your eyes and actions—not only in what you say. If there is any conflict between your words and your actions, however, persons will believe what you do—what you are rather than what you say. Your face and your actions can reflect true esteem for them. Your silent language can say, "You are important to me. I care about you."

L LISTENING AND PRAYER

istening, if sincere, is an act of affirming, healing, and encouraging. It is a personal gift of time that raises another person's self-esteem. We cannot overestimate the great need individuals have to be taken seriously, to be really heard, and to be understood. To survive, every human being must be heard and accepted by at least one person. Your ministry of listening is a precious gift of your time. It says to the person speaking, "You are important to me."

How another person listens tells me I'm either worthwhile or worth less. Should you yawn, look at your watch, or glance out the window while I'm sharing ideas significant to me, your actions suggest to me that you don't really care. Neither is it helpful if you cut in with advice or cliche-like answers while I'm struggling to express my feelings. You'll help me the most if you listen in silence—as an equal, not as a superior with ready-made remedies.

Prayer may be the ultimate affirmation. A business friend of mine was critically ill. He was still hospitalized when he received a long distance phone call from a United States senator whom he knew. The senator said that his office staff at morning meetings had been upholding him in prayer during his serious illness. But the senator did not stop at saying, "We have prayed *for* you." He prayed *with* my friend over the phone. As my friend reported the event, he reflected seriously, "His beautiful prayer in that unusual situation broke me up. I'll never forget it!"

My wife participates in our church prayer fellowship. Requests to remember those with special needs are systematically telephoned to all prayer members. Recently, I asked about the cause of my wife's tears. She replied that it was because a friend had passed away. Lois explained, "I have been upholding this lady in prayer over the past 14 months. She became a special friend through prayer even though I never met her."

We don't always feel adequate to pray acceptably for others, with others, or for ourselves. But Paul gives us hope in his writings to the Christians in Rome.

> ... the Spirit also comes to help us, weak that we are.
> For we do not know how we ought to pray; the Spirit
> Himself pleads with God for us, in groans that

words cannot express. And God, who sees into the hearts of men, knows what the thought of the Spirit is; because the Spirit pleads with God on behalf of His people and in accordance with His will (Rom. 8:26-27, TEV).

What an obvious evidence of God's concern for us to have the Holy Spirit plead on our behalf! What higher example is there for our concern of others?

8
Masking My Unacceptability

The less my self-confidence, the greater my need to wear masks.

THE DEMANDS OF PERFECTIONISTS

Parents usually want their children to be "better" than they were. We hope youth will not repeat our foolish mistakes. Regardless of our child's achievements, some of us are never satisfied. If a report card shows five "A's" and one "B," we dwell on the "B" and probe into "What went wrong?" In such circumstances children evaluate themselves as constantly falling short of our expectations. Even when working to their maximum ability, youth can feel inadequate and believe that anything short of flawlessness is unacceptable. In effect, we are criticizing them for not being perfect. But if our children were perfect, what would they think of us?

When others have unreasonable expectations of me, I feel a need to project a "front" of success. Then others will think of me as someone who "has it made." But such a mask frustrates friends who compare what they know of themselves with what they see on my deceptive and falsely positive mask.

WHAT WILL THE NEIGHBORS THINK?

When I was a child a dear neighbor known as Auntie Mikle lived in the house across the back fence. Without her knowledge, Auntie Mikle became a major controlling influence in my life. When my parents wanted my behavior to improve, they asked me, "What would Auntie Mikle think of what you just did?" The query of "what will the neighbors think?" supplanted my personal judgments. Over a period of time I hid my genuine self behind a mask that I thought the Auntie Mikles in my life would like to see.

Masking is a form of deception, first of others who don't know the real me—but more seriously, it becomes self-deception. Eventually I was plagued with the worry that others might not like the real me. I had become an echo of other people's expectations. The outgrowth of this process is self-rejection, a concern that my real self is unacceptable—to me, to family, to friends, to God. I had surrendered myself to a whittling down process to fit better the expectations of others.

Because it was an effective method of control, "What will the neighbors think?" became one of my parents' frequently used tapes. The self-denying consequences of wearing masks, however, are damaging when they impair selfconfidence.

As a form of insincerity, masking can be exhausting. We sap our energy to keep up false appearances. Masking drains the participant who worries, "Would my friends like the real me, or are they just friends of my mask?" Normally the less confident a person feels, the more he needs a mask. Also, the more authoritative or domineering the external mask, the greater the hidden feelings of insecurity.

Masks are barriers to honest relationships. Masks can't communicate; only individuals can. The more I need to use protective barriers, the more I conceal my real identity. I am less authentic and therefore less understandable to others.

Early in my career I was a new and inexperienced vice-principal in a high school of 2,000 students. Among other duties, I was accountable for the discipline of 1,000 active young men—no trivial challenge to a perfectionist. I discovered that the less secure I felt, the more exacting I became. To cover up my fears and inadequacies, I erred on the side of strictness rather than leniency.

On one occasion, student notices of a coming "G-day" had been posted around the school. Since the school name was Grant and its nickname "The Generals," I made no immediate investigation of the coming event. On "G-day" I was disconcerted to learn that the signs referred to "Gangster Day." Fortunately for my composure, Reuben, our student body president, offered to assist. We worked together to confiscate everything from cap pistols and water pistols to genuine German Lugers carried by the more enterprising students.

One tall basketball player was among those dressed as a gangster. He wore an old derby slanted over one eye. I found him standing by his open hall locker. When I asked him to store the derby during school hours, he glowered defiantly at me. I questioned momentarily whether I had the self-confidence to confront him. But I was young and energetic. My authority had been challenged. I couldn't afford to lose face. With my most convincing mask, I reached up, took off his derby, stuffed it into the locker and slammed the door. I wasn't sure whether I too might get stuffed in the locker, but his defiance folded. Mask A had out-maneuvered Mask B, but there had been little person to person relationship.

COMMUNICATION OF DESPERATION

Suicide is a language of desperation, an ultimate communique that demands attention. There is no way the message can be ignored.

There were 28,100 suicides reported in the United States in 1981. Twenty percent (5,650 individuals) were under 24 years of age, triple the rate of 1974.

Each day 18 American adolescents die by suicide. The real number probably is higher due either to erroneous or intentional under-reporting. Some experts claim there are two or three suicides for every one recorded. Dr. J. Vernon Magnuson of the Emory University School of Medicine claims that suicidal attempts among teenagers occur 50 times more frequently than suicidal deaths.

Authorities agree that youth driven to suicide feel unrelated, ignored, and unloved. One youth who attempted suicide said later that he was convinced that no one cared for him as a human being.

Think for a while about the agonizing feelings of desperation, loneliness, guilt, self-renunciation, and shat-

67

tered self-esteem associated with a person considering self-destruction! The discouragement and hopelessness that prompt a youth to take his life are based on very personal perceptions. It is possible that the individual may not have been as completely neglected as he feels, but his *feelings are genuine to him.* Probably no family member or friend has gone out of his or her way to assure the individual that he is wanted, cared for, or important to them.

Those who feel that life has no meaning for them and those who have lost all hope feel worthless. They are starving for evidence that someone cares what happens to them. They need to know they are important to their family, community, or church. Most of all they need to hear that God cares for them, unconditionally.

Frequently we offer only conditional love. We say, in effect, "You will have our love *if* you are a top student, an outstanding athlete, an accomplished musician." But it is difficult to maintain a reasonable sense of self-worth when someone important in your life is disappointed daily because you have not come up to their standards.

Our nation's top colleges have an above average suicide rate. Academic competition is great. Expectations of family and friends are even greater. Suicides tend to occur among the more capable students who *should* be feeling more self-confident. Yet one university student felt crushed. He explained, "I let my family down. I was only second in my class!"

Jesus' second commandment tells us to love our neighbor as we love ourselves (Matt. 22:37, TEV). It is a difficult paradox for many of us to accept. I need adequate self-confidence and self-esteem before I can share these with my neighbor. But it's difficult to give my neighbor the love needed for his self-esteem until I have accepted God's unconditional love and acceptance.

My relationship to God has some effect on the world's suicide rate. If I fail to accept God's love and forgiveness, my self-esteem wobbles. I become insecure and fearful as I try to go it alone. I repudiate myself as I put on masks to hide my fragile self-image. Disregarding God's plan of salvation, I flounder in self-depreciation. I am in no condition to love, support, encourage, or praise my neighbor.

It is a great relief to drop my mask and admit to God that I am another imperfect member of His human race in continual need of His boundless love. When I am reconciled to God through His gracious forgiveness I am better able to love my neighbor as myself. This is an example of God's generous gift which Paul speaks of in his second letter to the Christians at Corinth. He says for all who are hurting that "in Christ God was reconciling the world to Himself, . . . and . . . entrusting to us the message of reconciliation" (5:19).

9
Reluctance to Affirm or Accept Affirming

Persons often have positive feelings
they find difficult to express.
Merle M. Ohlsen

I have yet to find a person who will not put forth more sustained effort under a positive spirit of appreciation than under a negative spirit of criticism. Why, then, do we take good work for granted—but not with gratitude? Most lives are barren not because so many bad things happen, but because so few good things happen.

TOO LITTLE AND TOO LATE

For a number of years I have studied audience reaction following a speech or some other public performance. A speaker normally invests numerous hours or days to develop an excellent presentation. My analysis reveals, however, that one percent or less of audiences ever expresses any appreciation for even the best talks.

Some individuals praise very moderately. Faint praise is a disparagement. Dr. Merle Ohlsen has written to me, "I find that persons often have positive feelings which they are reluctant or unable to express. As a result, they lose many opportunities to develop or enrich a relationship."

Our unwillingness to affirm others robs them of oxygen for their souls. When we withhold deserved praise, we contribute to psychological malnutrition. Insecure persons uncertain of God's love may need extra affirmation to help

71

them comprehend a divine love that changes lives. And our actions toward others need to be consistent with our words lest they be considered hollow.

My uncle's funeral was typical of many I have attended. There was a beautiful affirmative eulogy, but the words seemed too late. His commendable qualities and assistance to others were lauded in the formal service and recognized by individuals in informal groups afterwards. The comments were appropriate and true. But why don't we grant equal affirmation time to those still living? Tomorrow often is too late.

THE TROUBLE WITH GETTING PRAISE

*A*t an in-service session, teachers had been encouraged to phone parents of their students and report on positive behavior. Later that week a teacher phoned a student's home, reached the mother, and began to share something commendable that her son, Bill, had done in class. Soon the mother rejected the call with a blunt, "You've got the wrong number!" Surprised, the teacher did some more checking. Soon both mother and teacher realized they were talking about the same boy. At that point the mother broke down and cried. She sobbed, "No one has ever phoned from school unless there was some problem. Thank you so much for taking the time to share this positive information!"

Sometimes we reject affirmations because so much of what we have experienced in life has been negative. In addition, we are often guilty of putting our own selves down.

There are understandable reasons why we reject appreciations. For example, I can still hear my parents warning me against anything that even closely resembled pride. They wanted me to avoid arrogance and conceit. But their warnings had far-reaching effects. Feelings have persisted that I did not amount to much—that people could not like the real me. When someone would praise me, one of my immediate responses would be:

    (a) "Oh, it was nothing." (This was a common phrase among Scandinavians.)

    (b) That person is flattering me for some reason. I

72

should be cautious until I discover what he really wants.

(c) She's just wanting to be kind. She can't mean what she says.

(d) He's not knowledgeable enough to judge what I've done; hence, his evaluation is not well founded.

(e) She doesn't know me well. If she *really* knew about me, she'd know I'm not worthy of such affirmations.

Such reactions contradict the affirmer and frustrate a sincere attempt to be kind and loving. In addition, I felt obliged to "pay back" for the affirmation so I would no longer be "in debt" to my benefactor. A feeling of indebtedness destroyed the true joy that should be associated with receiving. God's love, however, suggests that my best response is to accept the affirming gift with joy and thanksgiving.

Several new understandings have helped me grow and mature in regard to accepting affirmations and gifts.

(a) The act of giving inevitably grants joy to the giver also. ("It is more blessed to give than to receive" [Acts 20:35].) To disaffirm a gift by whatever means is to blockade the blessing due the giver.

(b) Where a relationship exists between two persons, one of them will not feel affirmed if he is always the recipient of gifts or help, and the second person continually rejects all offers of assistance.

(c) While Jesus gave of Himself regularly, He was able to receive as well. He had no home of His own. He rode on a borrowed donkey. Others buried Him in a borrowed tomb. He granted to others the satisfaction of being helpful.

(d) Everyone needs to experience the joy and blessing of being able to give and having others accept the help gracefully.

Part of my difficulty in accepting affirmations and gifts from others was related to a faulty understanding of God's love. For years I found it difficult to believe that I was truly acceptable to a heavenly Father until I could accept what Christ had done for me. Then I realized that someone who throughout childhood felt unaccepted and worthless to a parent would have difficulty reversing feelings of low self-esteem overnight. Finally I realized there is no way I can pay God back for His gift of salvation. Gifts must be accepted as gifts—with joy, thanksgiving, and praise.

Corrie Ten Boom tells of the beautiful way she accepts affirmations. In *God's Best for My Life* Lloyd John Ogilvie describes his conversation with her. He asked how she handles the compliments and adulation she receives from people. She answered;

> ... that is no problem. Every time a person praises me for something I've done, I just accept it as a flower. Then at the end of the day I put all the flowers together into a lovely bouquet, get on my knees, and say, "Here, Father, this bouquet belongs to you! The lovely things people have said about me, they were really saying about You. Thank You, Father, for using me."[1]

10
The Work World– Infirming

You can do twenty years of right and one hour of wrong and they'd string you.
Studs Terkel

Many supervisors seem unaware of William James's insight that the deepest need of human nature is to be appreciated. Workers protest that supervisors fail to acknowledge *any* contribution made, however large or small. Workers who are denied feedback are ignorant of how well they are doing in their work. Studies report that good workers regress and become only average workers when ignored.

Many of our nation's workers suffer from an unseen malnutrition. They are starved for recognition and praise. A supervisor's reluctance to acknowledge good work is a costly oversight. (In this chapter, the term "supervisor" will be used to mean all leadership positions, whether in local communities, congregations, or the many different managerial levels found in the work world.)

Praise and recognition, when sincere and merited, boost morale and output. If a leader praises an individual or a group when not deserved, workers see the affirmation as hollow flattery and of no significance.

Supervisors normally fall into one of two major categories—basement people or balcony people. Basement people are habitually negative. They lack confidence in subordinates, see them as incompetent. Balcony people are habitually positive. They hold high expectations for workers, see them as capable, listen to them and express both recognition and praise. Supervisors need to realize that affirming the good things workers do is infinitely more productive than disregarding their accomplishments. Someone has said: "The formula for success is putting the right people in the right jobs and then sitting on the sidelines and being a rousing good cheerleader!"

NEGLECTING APPRECIATION FOR GOOD WORK

Supervisors who disregard the capable worker will soon discover that employees resent having their good work ignored. Studies reveal that most supervisors misinterpret which job conditions employees consider most important.

The National Labor Relations Institute completed a "job condition study" in 1946. One of the 10 factors included in the survey was "Appreciation for good work." Workers ranked this as most important to them. Supervisors ranked the 10 factors as they thought workers would prioritize them. Supervisors ranked "appreciation for good work" as eighth in importance to workers! The factor that workers ranked second was "feeling of being in on things"—being kept informed by management. Supervisors estimated that workers would rank it ninth.

How can leaders be so ignorant regarding the importance of positive interpersonal relationships? The job condition study was repeated by George Mason University in 1979. I anticipated that the results 33 years later would show a more enlightened leadership. Workers did select "interesting work" as number one. But "full appreciation for good work" was their second choice. Supervisors, however, still believed employees would rank appreciation for good work eighth in importance. This misconception about workers and their needs continues basically unchanged a third of a century later.

Hearing this, defensive supervisors at some of my management seminars have responded, "But if I don't criticize persons, they know I appreciate what they do." The absence of criticism and the ignoring of good work will never substitute for deserved appreciation and praise.

There is a story of a man in a drugstore making a phone call. "Mr. Johnson?" he said. "I hear that you have been looking for an office manager." He paused. "Oh, you hired one two months ago and you're very satisfied. Well, thank you anyway." When he stepped out of the phone booth the druggist commented, "I wasn't trying to eavesdrop, but I overheard your conversation. I'm sorry you didn't get the job." "Oh, that's all right," the man replied smiling. "That's my boss. I'm his office manager. I was just phoning to find out how I'm doing!" Do your workers, family members, or church members need to resort to a ruse to learn how you feel about their performance?

POOR COMMUNICATING, POOR LISTENING

*I*n the work world there usually is minimal communication by the supervisor about organizational goals, objectives, and priorities. Many individuals also hesitate to ask for needed information. They feel it may be a sign of weakness. Yet the greater our responsibilities, the more we need to ask associates for help. It's a mistake to assume that we will appear weak. Being openly helpable is a positive interactive technique. Approach both superiors and subordinates with, "I need your help. Can you tell me....?" Not only will we learn more; we will also affirm those contacted by recognizing them as persons able to be of assistance.

Employees often need the uninterrupted attention of their leaders. Studies indicate that while supervisors spend about 40 percent of their days listening, they usually comprehend only one-third of what they hear. Competent leaders will repeat, in their own words, the core of what another person says and check their understanding of the communication's central theme.

Sperry Corporation has completed some interesting studies in the field of listening. On a scale of zero to 100 (with 100 being high), most persons rated themselves at the 55th percent level as listeners. That is below "failing" in any normal grading system.

The Sperry study found that individuals felt they listened to their supervisors and best friends at a rate *above* 55 percent. Listening to their associates and subordinates was rated at the 55 percent level. But listening to one's spouse was scored *below* 55 percent—and the score continued to fall the more years one had been married. The ministry of listening is a powerful and affirming tool when used in love.

On the other hand, workers resent being uninformed. A supervisor's failure to share information results in workers being ignorant. Of necessity they finally respond to inquiries with, "Don't ask me, I just work here." This knowledge vacuum spoils good morale and causes workers to feel worth less. A considerate leader meets with workers regularly, reviews current objectives, explains changes in priorities, and responds to questions. The effective leader also asks, "What am I doing that cramps your style?" and "What am I doing that you could do for me?"

I encountered a dismal situation in one office when a capable secretary to an executive let off some steam with these comments:

He's in his office with the door closed, practically tearing his hair out with all the work piled up before him—and I'm sitting out here with time to help him. But he's too busy to sit down and talk with me. I might as well not be a member of his team.

Supervisors are shortsighted when they get too busy to talk with and listen to their workers. Frequently communication in organizations is "one-way"—down from the top. Leaders listen too little to the workers who generally know the most about operational details. Workers' suggestions for improvement are far more valuable than we realize.

DEAF TO NON-VERBAL COMMUNICATION?

*W*hen there is a contradiction between what a leader says and does, workers will believe the supervisor's actions. For example, I may claim that customer courtesy is the number one priority of our organization. But if I am rude to customers, the worker reaction will be, "What you do speaks so loud, I can't hear what you say!"

Once I worked in an organization that treated professional staff members as unimportant workhands. With a disdainful attitude, superiors shifted staff members from one location to another. They uprooted whole departments on the pretext of needing space, which later was grossly underutilized. When planning to remodel, the supervisors failed to consult the persons who were to work in the new area. As a result, the space allocations and traffic patterns were poorly planned. More serious, worker morale plummeted because of management's arrogant attitude. Workers felt ignored and worthless. Staff attitudes ranged for from unenthusiastic to belligerent. Management's actions said to the workers on whom they depended to complete their work, "We could care less how you feel!"

INDIFFERENCE BY SUPERVISORS

The seminar I was presenting on "Humane Management" had been in session for about two hours. Participants were busily involved on a lab activity when the chief executive of the organization arrived. Looking like Napoleon, he strutted in, surveyed the activity, spotted a particular participant and blurted out, "Well, I see you've got old Fred working today. Good for you. That's the first work Fred's done in three years!" The boss "put down" Fred in front of the whole staff. It was no laughing matter for Fred. I recalled one of the comments on a pre-seminar questionnaire about the organization's staff meetings. An employee had written, "When we meet together, someone is usually humiliated!" Then I realized why the planning committee had requested a conference on the topic of "humane management"!

Several California school administrators took part in a study to find the ratio of positive to negative statements overheard in school staff rooms. They visited 32 schools throughout the nation. Study-team members sat in staff lounges and listened to employee comments. They counted the number of positive and negative comments. I assumed there would be more negative thoughts. I was shocked that the ratio was only six percent positive and 94 percent negative. The results challenge all leaders. They verify a crying need to accentuate the positive, express sincere appreciation, and engage in sincere two-way communication.

By nature, we seem to have an overdeveloped vocabulary for criticism and blame. At the same time we have a limited vocabulary for appreciation and praise. Workers like to hear positive statements from leaders such as "Excellent idea!" "Just what we need!" "That's planning ahead!" and "I need your advice." But it seems easier to say "That will never do," "You're late again," "That's an outrageous request!" or "Why don't you think of those things in advance?" Our human nature can identify with Paul when he said, "I do not understand what I do; for I don't do what I would like to do, but instead I do what I hate" (Rom. 7:15, TEV).

In his book, *Working,* Studs Terkel tells of a stock chaser who had worked in the Ford Motor Company for 23 years. He commented, "You can do twenty years of right and one hour of wrong and they'd string you."[1] It is a substantial challenge to remember, let alone live according to Paul's admonition when he says, ". . . fill your mind with those things that are good and deserve praise. . . ." (Phil. 4:8, TEV).

A supervisor's insensitivity to the work load or the working conditions of employees is inhumane. Most of my superiors have been concerned about any work overload. Therefore, one exception I experienced really stands out.

I found working for an insensitive, steam-roller type supervisor could vary from frustrating to devastating. I decided a conference with my supervisor was needed when I was asked to take on more responsibilities while already working over 50 hours a week. When I was told "nothing can be dropped nor can any current tasks be deferred," I was discouraged and frustrated. Everyone suffers from such an infirming approach—the employee, organizational morale, and eventually the supervisor.

We shouldn't overlook one positive side to working for an indifferent supervisor. I have heard that such bosses are never completely without merit; they always can serve as horrible examples.

There are many ways that supervisors may infirm workers. After calling a group together for a meeting, the leader can accept unscheduled interruptions such as phone calls. He forgets that those who have traveled a distance to attend his meeting at a predetermined hour are forced to sit idly by. This is inconsiderate as well as an expensive waste of time. The leader's action says to those assembled, "You are worth less than the unscheduled phone call I have allowed to interrupt."

Some words of Jesus are relevant for all leaders.

The kings of the Gentiles lord it over them; . . . But you are not to be like that. Instead, the greatest among you should be like the youngest, and the one who rules like the one who serves (Luke 22:25-26, NIV).

11
The Work World–Affirming

The applause of a single human being is of great consequence.
Samuel Johnson

SATISFYING THE NEED FOR APPRECIATION

As a high school principal, I began a practice of writing notes of thanks, appreciation, and congratulations to teachers, students, and parents. While any plain paper is appropriate, I used special paper with "Congratulations" or "Thank you" printed at the top.

Positive recognition is always welcome and boosts the recipient's self-esteem. Fifteen years after leaving the principalship I learned about the lasting effects of documented appreciation. A retired teacher informed me that she had kept each of the notes of appreciation I had written to her. Two weeks later I was talking with a former student to whom I had written notes of congratulations. He reported having kept the affirmative notes written many years before. Identical reactions from two different sources surprised me. Then I recalled that I have a file folder at home which contains some affirmative notes received over the years. But I haven't saved one check stub for all those years!

It seems that we often are more lavish when praising those we know least well. We are less considerate with those who do our work. And we're least generous with praise to those who are nearest and dearest.

A man who attended a seminar on interpersonal relations realized his failure to tell his wife how much he treasured her. So he bought some candy and flowers to redeem himself. Once home he rang the doorbell. His wife opened the door, looked at him, and broke out crying. He asked what was wrong. She replied, "Everything went wrong today! The washing machine broke down; Bill fell off his bicycle and skinned his knee; the dog broke out the screen in the front door; and now you come home drunk!" Someone has suggested that we try praising family members even if it frightens them at first.

DELEGATION PROCLAIMS TRUST

If it were considered desirable to destroy a human being, the only thing necessary would be to give his work a character of uselessness. Dostoevsky

Non-verbal communication can express trust or lack of trust as effectively as words. When a supervisor stops talking to an employee, it often is a sign of lost confidence. Instead of talking over the problem, a supervisor often takes back work previously delegated.

Failure to delegate responsibility shows a low trust level in the worker or a feeling of indispensability by the supervisor. If a leader will only challenge workers with greater responsibilities, workers tend to be more enthusiastic. Low-trust leaders are forever looking over the worker's shoulder, ready to recall the responsibility at the first sign of a problem. This destroys the challenge of any position.

One of the paradoxes in management is that prophecy tends to generate its own fulfillment. When supervisors treat employees as if they were unreliable or unwilling to cooperate, workers will respond in that way. Low morale and resistance cause the entire organization to suffer.

I was principal of a city high school for years. Without fail, the level of trust I exhibited in student body leaders was an accurate prediction of their actions. In 10 years, I don't recall one instance when executive council members failed to live up to my high expectations and expressed confidence.

The student body also reacted positively to the faculty's challenge and trust. Our high school was the only one in the city that scheduled a 12-minute snack break between second and third periods each day. No student was to leave campus during the break. Neither was any staff member assigned to enforce compliance. Students knew they were trusted with this special privilege. They also knew that if they abused the trust they would lose the privilege. Students effectively counseled any careless classmate who endangered their privilege.

The student body also knew that our administration considered assemblies a privilege, not a right. Neither students nor teachers had an assigned seat during assemblies. Teachers were not expected to be on duty; students were responsible for their own good conduct. And students rose to the challenge!

One assembly program by the Portland Symphony Orchestra was a great event for the students. It wasn't the classical music that thrilled them. The triumph was in their praiseworthy conduct. The students knew I had been under faculty pressure to tighten up assembly control "just to be safe." They also knew I had refused to lower my expectations and trust. When the assembly was over the symphony conductor asked to speak to the students. He told them that in all the orchestra's previous high school appearances, no group had reacted in such a mature and appreciative manner. The students were exultant! Symphony day became the source of increased pride and new maturity for the students and their leaders. Faculty members praised them for the exemplary way they had responded. We let the parents know of our pride in the maturity level of the students. I believe the individual and group esteem was higher after the symphony assembly than when the basketball team won the state tournament. Each student had been an indispensable part of the success.

We have numerous opportunities to affect positively the lives of others by our high expectations and by the level of trust we place in them.

PRAISE AND A POSITIVE CLIMATE

Employee negotiations typically center on wages and benefits. Appreciation for good work is not measurable and is usually ignored. Is that one reason supervisors give so little attention to praising their workers?

Why are many leaders reluctant to utilize such a positive influence? Samuel Johnson assures us that "The applause of a single human being is of great consequence." Leaders can help workers grow by reinforcing improvements in their work with praise.

Charles Schwab was one of the first millionaires. He was not successful because of his technical knowledge but because of his effective interpersonal and human relations skills. He has said,

> I consider my ability to arouse enthusiasm among the men the greatest asset I possess, and the way to develop the best that is in a man is by appreciation and encouragement. . . . So I am anxious to praise but loathe to find fault. If I like anything, I am hearty in my appreciation and lavish in my praise.

Supervisors will encourage and affirm workers if they:
  (a) communicate regularly the organization's changing objectives and priorities.
  (b) invite new ideas from the workers. There are better ways to do every task.
  (c) prepare a "daily do" list with all items ranked in order of importance.
  (d) trust workers by delegating responsibilities that give growth opportunities.
  (e) check with employees to determine what extra time or equipment they need. Work to provide these.
  (f) be fair to all. Playing favorites undermines morale.
  (g) be a good example. Model the work qualities you preach.
  (h) praise each employee for any job well done: orally is okay, in writing is better.
  (i) move around the organization to meet with the workers. Initiate the greeting; workers may feel reticent to do so.

Sincere praise establishes a climate that reduces employee stress. It is rewarding to *know* that you are doing a good job and that you are promoting the organization's goals in an effective way. People who are recognized feel a stronger commitment to the organization.

Improved communication and sincere appreciation have

a positive effect on workers. They enhance self-esteem, reduce stress, increase commitment, and heighten job satisfaction. All of these increase productivity—at a relatively low cost.

The author of the following poem is unknown. I have paraphrased portions of the poem to adapt it today's work world.

If I Were Leader

If I were leader I'd like to say:
"You did an excellent job today."
I'd look for a man, or woman or boy
Whose heart would leap with a thrill of joy
At a word of praise, and I'd pass it out
Where others could hear what I talked about.

If I were a leader I'd like to find
The person whose work is the proper kind;
And whenever to me a good thing came
I'd like to be told the toiler's name,
And I'd go to the person who had toiled to win,
And I'd say, "That was perfectly splendid, Lynn!"

Now a bit of praise isn't much to give,
But it's dear to the hearts of all that live;
For there's never a person on this old earth
But is glad to know that one's been of worth;
And a kindly word, when the work is fair,
Is welcome and wanted everywhere.

If I were leader I'm sure I would
Say a kindly word whenever I could;
For those who have given their best by day
Want a little more than their weekly pay.
They like to know, with the setting sun,
That the leader's pleased with the work they've done.

We all need praise and affirmation. Fortunately, God who takes note of every sacrifice and service is not loathe to praise His children. In a parable about what the kingdom of heaven can be compared to, Jesus concludes with the Master's comment to one of His servants, "Well done, good and faithful servant! You have been faithful with a few things; I will put you in charge of many things. Come and share your master's happiness!" (Matthew 25:21, NIV).

12
Live What You Believe

*The deeds you do may be the only sermon
some persons will hear today.*
St. Francis

When a high school principal, I was given the following summary of an English paper written by a student.

We are taught to be peaceful in an agitated world.

We are taught to be moral; yet we are aware of immorality.

We are taught to have respect for law and order in a society torn by rioting.

We are told to study by those who play.

We are criticized for seeking popularity by a conforming society.

We are told to work by those who deny us jobs.

We are told to be responsible by those who are irresponsible.

We admit we are a bit confused by the world around us.

Teaching and preaching have their place. But *living* God's love is the indispensable companion of *believing* Christ's Gospel. For better or for worse, our lives are the church's visible message. Where there are contradictions between what we say and what we do, the world will reject our Sunday statements and believe our weekday actions.

If we model our beliefs, we will serve as examples for others. Youth sorely need exemplary Christian models for their lives. The most effective guidance we can ever give them is how we live.

When we present a front of perfectionism while masking our real self, we construct a misleading model for our

89

associates. If we wish to help those who struggle with fears, disappointments, and guilt, we need to be honest enough to remove our masks and admit that we are strugglers also burdened with fears, disappointments, and guilt. We help others most by revealing our real selves, by confessing that our help is found in God's complete acceptance of us as we are—not as we would like to appear. Paul says, "My strength is made perfect in weakness" (2 Corinthians 12:9). We frustrate others when we wear a mask that falsely claims, "I've got it all together!" But we can help fellow seekers grow when they know we, too, are struggling human beings who know both joy and sorrow.

While the most effective way to change our community is to start with ourselves, it is much more tempting and less threatening to try to change others. Over 500 years ago Thomas a Kempis wrote: "Gladly we desire to make other men perfect but we will not amend our own fault." It is still true. We find it easier to criticize others than to be correct ourselves.

Teachers have an opportunity to model the type of affirmative behavior they desire in their classrooms. One teacher said that he began each new school year with three statements. First, he told his students, "I love you." Second, "I will not abuse you or allow anyone else to abuse you." Third, "I will not take abuse from you."

This teacher's practical philosophy was consistent with Christ's second commandment, "You shall love your neighbor as yourself" (Matt. 22:39). The teacher emphasized that he cherished his own self-esteem too much to let others tyrannize or humiliate him. At the same time, he also cherished each student's welfare to the extent that he would neither abuse them nor let another person do so.

This teacher also held high expectations for each student *and* expressed continual confidence that each could meet his expectations. He maintained that one way to subvert self-esteem was to expect too little. So he sought out, built on, and praised each student's strengths. He summarized his motivation technique as "behaving the way I expect others to behave." This is modeling at its best.

There are many examples of affirming acts that could serve as models of appropriate behavior. Our society, however, gives primary attention to sensational and perverse news. In fact, our media engulf us with poor behavior models. It is really amazing that each new generation turns out as well as it does with all the pathetic adult examples from which to learn.

Regardless how barren of talent some persons feel, everyone has special strengths. We may have to look carefully—even become sleuths—but we can find assets to recognize in everyone. We can help uncover these abilities, especially if not previously recognized, and help others improve their self-esteem.

Leo Bustad, Dean Emeritus of Veterinary Medicine at Washington State University, tells of his meeting with a man named Richard in Bethel, a community for seriously handicapped persons in Bielefeld, West Germany. Richard is a spastic who has great difficulty speaking and has had to spend all his life flat on his back. He appears to be a person without any usable gift. Leo Bustad shared the following summary:

> One of the most important things we must learn to do is to listen to those who are hard to listen to. On one of my trips to Europe I made a side trip to Bethel in Bielefeld, West Germany. I went there because I was told it was the most remarkable place in the world. Bethel means "City of God." It started in 1867 when some people in Westphalia decided that attics and backrooms were not the appropriate place to keep the retarded and the epileptics; so they founded a community and lived with the handicapped in this community. Today there are more than five thousand people there who are disadvantaged and over five thousand to take care of, live with, and have compassion for them.
>
> It was obvious during my visit there that they wanted me to meet Richard. He's the fellow I'm going to tell you about because he's the kind of person that, if you saw him some distance away, you would probably seek to avoid him because he's a spastic. He has no control over his voluntary muscles, and he grimaces when he talks, and he's hard to listen to. He caught sight of me when I entered the place where he lived; he wondered who I was. They told him I was from America, and on

hearing this, he became very excited because some Americans with compassion had been there and worked with him. He has spent his entire fifty-six years flat on his back. When he learned that I was a veterinarian, he became exceedingly excited; he began questioning me. He asked if we ever took care of birds that were injured. Were we ever able to make them fly if they had broken wings? How do you give therapy to fish? His last question to me was: "Do you employ Indians in your school of veterinary medicine?" I thought that an unusual question, but I said we did since we have both kinds of Indians. I asked my host after I said goodbye to Richard which Indians he meant because Native Americans are very popular in West Germany. He said he meant Indians from India because he's very concerned about them. In fact, he said, Richard supports a little child in India. On hearing this I wondered if I heard him right. I had. "Yes," he said, "what I did not tell you is that Richard has control of his right foot, and some years ago he learned how to paint with his right foot. Using mirrors he paints very beautiful pictures. We sell these pictures and all the money goes to support a little child in India.

Richard is hard to forget. We may never know anyone who has fewer apparent gifts than Richard. His use of what little he has reminds me of the saying, "Where the heart is willing it will find a thousand ways; where it is unwilling it will find a thousand excuses." Richard's act of love is continuously coupled with another proverb which gnaws at my conscience: "To whom much is given, much will be expected."

Evidently God's love in action at Bethel has transformed Richard's life. How else could he give his meager earnings to support another unfortunate person halfway around the world—someone he will never see? What an example for those of us who complain that we have no talents or abilities and no way to help those in need.

God's love is the primary inspiration for Richard, and for each of us. Jesus spent His life affirming the lonely, the guilt-ridden, the sick, the crippled, the oppressed. He affirms us today with a complete cancellation of our sins, accepting and loving us as we really are and not what we pretend to be.

He continues to affirm each of us with, "My grace is sufficient for you"—pastor, parishioner, prostitute, pianist, parent, or politician. He decrees that we model His love, forgiveness, and acceptance right where we live, where we work, where we play, where we worship, emboldened by His promise, ". . . lo, I am with you always, even to the end of the age."

If Richard is important in God's grand plan, so are we. We all experience times of frustration, times of defeat, and times of low self-esteem. Yet each of us has some God-given abilities and talents too long buried that need resurrection.

In his book *There's a Lot More to Health Than Not Being Sick,* Bruce Larson says that Jesus sees us not as we physically appear to others but as we really are inside. In spite of our sins, our failures, or our physical condition, Jesus sees the treasure His Spirit has planted in us and wants to call it forth. God continually calls us to see in others the true, the real, but often the hidden gifts. Life has no greater adventure than for us to be in partnership with God in loving and helping to make the people we contact realize they are important to us—and important to God.

Regardless of our present condition, we can join with Richard and the psalmist in the highest form of praise.

Praise the Lord, all nations!
Praise him, all peoples!
His love for us is strong, and his faithfulness is
eternal.
Praise the Lord!
(Psalm 117, TEV)

13
Love, the Leaven of all Affirmations

Love . . . always perseveres.
Love never fails.
1 Corinthians 13: 76-78 (NIV)

The topic of love initially was not part of this book's outline. Authors discover that once conceived, however, a book develops a life and a will all its own. Love persisted, and love won its place in this manuscript.

From studies of homeless infants, some loved and some ignored, we know that affirming care is essential for normal emotional growth. Similarly, children and adults must have affirming love for balanced emotional development.

Most of us could never think of physically destroying another person. Yet we are more careless about wounding another person emotionally. We would not withhold food or water needed to sustain physical existence were these in our power to give. But we can thoughtlessly withhold the love necessary to nurture emotional or spiritual well-being even when it is in our power to give. Lack of affection among persons dear to us inflicts deep hurts and scars. We can splinter the self-esteem of other individuals simply by ignoring them and their strengths. But we can also nourish their self-esteem if we will be used as channels of God's love.

We know that adults who were scarred by a lack of love in their childhood tend to repeat a similar scarring pattern with their children. Opportunities exist in every community to share God's love—the power needed to break the chain of infirming that handicaps multitudes of youth from one generation to another. It is essential that all children be *convinced* they are loved by their parents as well as by other adults in the church family.

Paul has written an affirming proclamation in 1 Corinthians 13:4-7:

> Love is patient, love is kind. It does not envy, it does not boast, it is not proud. It is not rude, it is not self-seeking, it is not easily angered, it keeps no records of wrongs. Love does not delight in evil but rejoices in the truth. It always protects, always trusts, always hopes, always perseveres. (NIV)

What a master plan for abundant living!

We may not expect an endorsement of Paul's thinking from a speaker at the World Psychiatric Congress. Yet at its annual meeting in Madrid, a major speaker stated, "Nonjudgmental, unconditional love is the most healing force in the world." God's unqualified love channeled to us through a friend can erode obstinate feelings of inferiority and guilt.

Recognizing my own acute need for love, why am I half-hearted about giving unconditional love to others? Do I avoid such commitments because there may be a price to pay? Will the needs of others interfere with my plans and impose on my personal time? Did Christ count the cost?

Aware of my self-centeredness, the apostle John would repeat his advice for early Christians and say to me, "Ken, by this we know love, that He laid down His life for us and we ought to lay down our lives for our sisters and brothers." God's love in Christ is our compelling model, not just of great love, but of unlimited, completely unconditional love—never merited on my part.

The only intentional transforming of persons I should attempt is self-improvement. I am tempted to become God's self-appointed volunteer for transforming others. It seems that I could be of substantial help by pointing out others' faults, but God does not need that kind of meddling in His affairs. He only asks that I live and *act* in love toward other persons, pray for them, and leave the task of transformation to Him.

Paul's example of love for his co-workers is a model for all. In Romans 16 he recognizes and appreciates their good work in a letter of personal greetings. He affirms his co-workers publicly with statements such as

> Priscilla and Aquila . . . risked their lives for me. I am grateful to them—not only I, but all the Gentile churches as well.
>
> Greetings to Mary, who has worked so hard for you.
>
> Greetings to Apelles, whose loyalty to Christ has been proved.
>
> Greetings to . . . Persis, who has done so much work for the Lord.
>
> Greetings to Rufus, that outstanding worker in the Lord's service, and to his mother, who has always treated me like a son (TEV).

We know from observations of life that those traits recognized and appreciated in individuals will be reinforced in them. Acknowledgment of both the obscure and the obvious contributions of God's servants encourages them with supportive love faithfully to continue their daily responsibilities.

14
Therefore...

I don't care how much you know,
I want to know how much you care.

*O*ur nation recently has demonstrated a heightened concern in providing for the physically handicapped. As they enter the mainstream of life, we become more conscious of their disabilities and needs. The same awareness does not exist today for those psychologically or emotionally handicapped. Usually there is little visible evidence of their infirmities.

Let's listen to comments by some human beings locked behind steel bars to illustrate this point. During a discussion one jail inmate said, "My dad had the 'lock him up' attitude. 'You're in there now and I'm not going to come and bail you out.' So now I won't talk to my dad and he wouldn't listen anyway."

Another inmate added, "My dad disowned me. He said, 'I don't want nothin' to do with you. Don't even come to see me when you come out. Don't write to me or call me . . . nothin'!' "

Many persons whose father or mother has rejected them suffer a profound handicap. They have great difficulty believing in the love and unconditional acceptance of a heavenly Father, who keeps reaching out and crying, "How many times have I wanted to put my arms around all your people, just as a hen gathers her chicks under her wings. . . ." (Matt. 22:37, TEV). Children and adults who have been rejected will need persistent and unconditional love from family or church members to help them comprehend and accept the love of God.

SOME NEW UNDERSTANDINGS

*I*nfirming experiences in childhood handicap us emotionally. The more persistent the void of early years, the greater our need to compensate for the loss in later life.

Persons we blame for our emotional handicaps possibly were similarly hurt in their youth. If such a person were spastic, we could see and accept the consequences of a physical handicap. Were we able to see an infirmed person's emotional handicap, his actions would be more understandable, possibly even acceptable. Love and forgiveness would more easily supplant the grudges that have burdened us for years.

If I love others as myself, I accept them as I do myself. If I reject myself, however, I tend to reject others. Consequently, I need to accept myself as God created me. I need no longer pretend to be something I am not. In fact, when I wear a mask that implies "I have it all together," my actions tend to imprison others in their own self-doubts. Honesty about myself can be my greatest gift to others. Then I can understand and support others in their daily struggles.

No matter how helpful I claim to be, I do not assist other persons by pointing out their faults—unless they have requested my evaluation. No other person will be exactly the same as you or me. When I fail to accept the God-given uniqueness of another, I engage in an unloving act of rejection.

As the Good Shepherd, Jesus seeks to find His own when they're lost. But let's not lose sight of another aspect of His ministry. Often Jesus did not travel out of his way to help individuals. He ministered to those he met along his daily travels. Our family, church, and work associates need to feel God's love incarnate in us during our "daily walks." They need both verbal and non-verbal evidences of our love. For God's sake, we should not take any of our associates "for granted."

When I become a transformed instrument of God's love I can best minister to the special needs of an infirmed person. My understanding the emotional needs of another, plus my love for the individual "just as he is," helps him grow toward self-acceptance. This is a prerequisite for freeing him to love as he is loved. As participants in God's redemptive work, the time we invest in caring for others may effect eternity. We never know how far our influence extends when we help someone encounter God's love and unconditional acceptance.

God's affirming acceptance and unconditional love bestow on every person the capacity to know self-esteem. We can unload formidable fears and inferior feelings at the foot of Christ's cross, leaving them there for eternity. We recieve the greatest affirmation possible from the most reliable source—God's complete acceptance and love. Do we need more than the promise, "You can throw the whole weight of your anxieties upn Him for you are His personal concern" (1 Peter 5:7, Phillips)? We come as we are. We know of His willingness to change us. Romans 12:2 proposes that we "let God transform us inwardly by a complete change of our minds."

J *SOME NEW CHALLENGES*

esus said, "Ask and you will receive" (Matt. 7:7, TEV). We must overcome personal pride which prevents our asking God and others for help. Jesus' model of leadership included asking persons for food, water, transportation, and fellowship. When I request assistance I admit the futility of trying to go it alone. I express confidence and trust in other persons. After receiving help, the appreciation I express is an added blessing to the helper.

Freely accept God's love incarnate in other individuals. Regardless of our unworthy feelings, others should find it easy, not toilsome, to help us. Refusing assistance denies others the happiness that comes with sharing. Rejecting help stifles their opportunity to experience God's paradoxical promise, "It's more blessed to give than to receive."

It is an inspiring challenge to become an agent of change in God's world plan. His acceptance frees us to help others grow in self-esteem. We become Chirst's associates, facilitating His goal of transforming lives by love. Our high expectations and confidence of what Christ can do in the lives of others helps release their potential, building trust both in God and in themselves. When we give others new responsibilities in the family, on the job, or in church, they develop life-transforming abilities of which they were previously unaware. Service builds self-confidence in the serving individuals. Our recognition and praise of such service heightens self-esteem.

If those who are hurting were to give us one reaction, it would be, "I don't care how much you know; I want to know how much you care!" Supportive love simply may mean your listening presence—saying nothing and just being there—sharing space and God's peaceful, voiceless love. Appropriate words, if any, may merely be, "I can't fully understand what is happening in your life, but I am upholding you in prayer each day."

When we receive God's unconditional forgiveness, His affirming love frees us to forgive and accept others. We no longer need to put down those we formerly saw as competitors. Now we can start accepting and building them up. Once God's love has conquered us, we should never minimize what He is able to do through us for others! He can transform us from infirming "basement persons" to affirming "balcony persons." Then we can help liberate and praise the talents and services of those with whom we live, work, and worship. This will release more of God's love in the world.

A close friend of our family recently was scheduled for a second brain operation. She phoned long distance and talked with my wife for some time. Her comments included, "Just in case I don't make it, I wanted your whole family to know I love them very much." Her thoughts were appreciated and consistent with Jesus' words, "This is my command: Love each other" (John 15:17, NIV).

Her phone call reminded me of something I recently read. It suggested that if all of us were suddenly aware that we only had a short time left to share what we really wished to say, every telephone booth and other means of communication in our nation would be jammed with persons rushing to declare their previously unexpressed love. Fortunately, the present still gives us that opportunity.

Is it possible that God is praised when we affirm, love, or praise our family and friends, our work associates, or even strangers? In Matthew Jesus said, "When you did it to one of these my brothers [and sisters], you were doing it to me" (25:40, TLB). The praise of our family and neighbors apparently is in harmony with our praise to God.

It is God's love that moves us to love one another, to look for hidden potentials, to encourage and praise, to increase the influence of good in the world. St. Paul never forgot the love of Christ whom he had once persecuted, but who had made of him a humble, caring, and loving apostle. What would the greatest apostle of all say to us who are similarly called and honored with the baptismal names of child, saint, and friend? Probably what he said in 1 Thessalonians:

> Therefore encourage one another and build each other up . . . encourage the timid, help the weak, be patient with everyone. Make sure that no one pays back wrong for wrong, but always try to be kind to each other and to everyone else (NIV).

Christ has put into the hands of His followers the power that changes lives, a power for good that leaves its mark on all generations. That power for good needs only to be unleashed to transform the lives of individuals, families, and nations. Who can do it but those who have experienced the power of the Good News in their lives, who have received the affirmation of God? If not you and me—who? If not today—when?

Introduction
1. Leo Buscaglia, *Living, Loving and Learning* (New York: Fawcett Columbine, 1982).

Chapter I
1. Joyce Landorf, *Irregular Persons* (Waco, Texas: Word Book Publishers, 1982).
2. Paul Tournier, *The Meaning of Persons* (New York: Harper and Row, 1957).
3. Alan Loy McGinnis, *The Friendship Factor* (Minneapolis: Augsburg Publishing House, 1979).
4. Bruce Larson, *Living on the Growing Edge* (Grand Rapids, Michigan: Zondervan Publishing House, 1968).

Chapter II
1. Nathaniel Branden, *The Disowned Self* (Los Angeles: Nash Publishing, 1971).
2. Lloyd John Ogilvie, *When God First Thought of You* (Waco, Texas: Word Book Publishers, 1978).

Chapter III
1. Paul Tournier, *The Strong and the Weak* (Philadelphia: Westminster Press, 1963).
2. Stephen Joseph, *The Me Nobody Knows* (New York: Avon Books, 1969).
3. J. N. Lenker, trans., *Luther's Large Catechism* (Minneapolis: Augsburg Publishing House, 1967).

Chapter VII
1. Bruce Larson, *Ask Me to Dance* (Waco, Texas: Word Book Publishers, 1972).

Chapter IX
1. Lloyd John Ogilvie, *God's Best for My Life* (Eugene, Oregon: Harvest House Publishers, 1981).

Chapter X
1. Studs Terkel, *Working* (New York: Avon Books, 1972).